Illicit Trade in High-Risk Sectors

IMPLICATIONS OF ILLICIT ALCOHOL FOR PUBLIC HEALTH AND CRIMINAL NETWORKS

OECD

BETTER POLICIES FOR BETTER LIVES

This document, as well as any data and map included herein, are without prejudice to the status of or sovereignty over any territory, to the delimitation of international frontiers and boundaries and to the name of any territory, city or area.

The statistical data for Israel are supplied by and under the responsibility of the relevant Israeli authorities. The use of such data by the OECD is without prejudice to the status of the Golan Heights, East Jerusalem and Israeli settlements in the West Bank under the terms of international law.

Please cite this publication as:
OECD (2022), *Illicit Trade in High-Risk Sectors: Implications of Illicit Alcohol for Public Health and Criminal Networks*, Illicit Trade, OECD Publishing, Paris, https://doi.org/10.1787/1334c634-en.

ISBN 978-92-64-50373-1 (print)
ISBN 978-92-64-71395-6 (pdf)

Illicit Trade
ISSN 2617-5827 (print)
ISSN 2617-5835 (online)

Foreword

Illicit trade is a universal threat that grows in scope and magnitude undermining good governance, the rule of law and citizens' trust in government. Illicit trade not only has a corrosive impact on the sales and profits of affected firms and on the economy in general, but also poses critical threats to social welfare, and public safety. In addition, in some high-risk sectors, such as that of illicit pharmaceuticals, food or alcohol, illicit trade poses particularly severe health and safety threats for citizens.

The pandemic has been fuelling these problems as for criminals and other bad actors that drive illicit trade networks, it has been an excellent opportunity to free ride on new possibilities. The key COVID-19-related elements that shape the dynamics of illicit trade in these high-risk sectors include the closure of borders, reshape of suppliers' structure, destruction of existing relations in supply chains, as well as the change in enforcement priorities. Corruption and insecurity continue to fuel illicit trade across markets and economies. Besides, these changes have been occurring very rapidly, leaving minimal scope for a reaction.

In recent years, the OECD has been gathering evidence on various aspects of this trade and the factors that enable it. The results have been published in a set of factual reports, including *Governance Frameworks to Counter Illicit Trade* (2017), *Trade in Counterfeit Pharmaceutical Products* (2020) and *Dangerous Fakes - Trade in Counterfeit Goods that Pose Health, Safety and Environmental Risks* (2022). In addition, during the pandemics the OECD organized a series of online webinar to scope the main areas of impact that the sanitary crisis has on illicit trade. The findings point at severe health and safety threats of illicit trade in some high-risk sectors, additionally augmented during the pandemic.

This report provides evidence on the illicit alcohol trade, as part of the work of the OECD Task Force on Countering Illicit Trade on sectors that are at high risk for illicit trade. The results are a cause for concern. Trade in illicit alcohol products is an attractive target for organised crime, as both the market and potential profits are large, in some cases requiring little investment. Importantly, illicit alcohol supplied by criminals is often substandard and poses very high health risks.

This study was carried out under the auspices of the OECD's Task Force on Countering Illicit Trade, which focuses on evidence-based research and advanced analytics to assist policy makers in mapping and understanding the vulnerabilities exploited by illicit trade.

Acknowledgements

This report was prepared by the OECD Public Governance Directorate (GOV), under the leadership of Elsa Pilichowski, Director, and Martin Forst, Head of the Governance Reviews and Partnerships Division.

The report was prepared by Morgane Gaudiau, Economist at the OECD Directorate for Public Governance and Peter Avery, Senior Consultant. Piotr Stryszowski, Senior Project Manager in Charge of the TF-CIT provided overall guidance. The authors wish to thank the OECD experts who provided valuable knowledge and insights: Julio Bacio Terracino and Carissa Munro and from the OECD Public Governance Directorate.

Andrea Uhrhammer and Ciara Muller provided editorial and production support.

The database on customs seizures was provided by the World Customs Organization (WCO) and supplemented with regional data submitted by the European Commission's Directorate-General for Taxation and Customs Union, the US Customs and Border Protection Agency and the US Immigration and Customs Enforcement. The authors express their gratitude for the data and for the valuable support of these institutions.

Table of contents

Tables

Boxes

Follow OECD Publications on:

http://twitter.com/OECD_Pubs

http://www.facebook.com/OECDPublications

http://www.linkedin.com/groups/OECD-Publications-4645871

http://www.youtube.com/oecdilibrary

http://www.oecd.org/oecddirect/

Executive summary

The market for alcohol products is an attractive target for illicit trade and organised crime as the market is large, as are the profits that can be made from the illicit trade, in some cases with little investment. The ease with which consumers can be deceived into buying illicit products, and the low risk of detection for all forms of illicit trade, create suitable conditions for eluding law enforcement.

This report i) provides an overview of the alcohol industry, ii) examines the nature and scope of illicit trade in the sector, iii) assesses the impacts of illicit trade on socio-economic development, iv) identifies the factors driving illicit trade in the sector, v) reviews the measures that stakeholders have taken to better understand and combat the illicit trade, and vi) provides an overview of some of the key issues that need to addressed to deal with the societal challenges posed by the illicit alcohol trade.

There are many types of illicit alcoholic beverages, including counterfeit goods (refilling, falsification and tampering); smuggled/contraband items that have been illegally imported into a jurisdiction and sold, evading import duties, taxes and customs formalities; illicit artisanal alcoholic beverages; legally produced alcohol beverages on which the required excise tax is not paid in the jurisdiction of production (tax leakage); and non-conforming alcohol products, including products not meant for human consumption.

The market for illicit alcohol is large. In 2018, the total consumption of alcohol worldwide equalled to 6.2 litres of pure alcohol per person 15 years and older and illicit alcohol accounted for about 25% of this volume, but disproportionately larger in lower-income countries. As a general rule, illicit alcohol trade is closely linked to the low affordability of products. First, a relatively low cost of producing illicit beverages means potentially high profits for illicit traders. For example, the fixed cost of producing illicit spirits can be quite low, which means the market is relatively open to both small- and large-scale operators. Second, governments tend to impose additional taxes on alcohol for a number of reasons, including public health objectives. At the same time, these taxes can create additional incentives for counterfeiters to enter the market and supply illicit alternatives outside the licit supply chain.

A principal challenge for large-volume illicit traders is infiltrating legitimate supply chains. Success in doing so often relies on the gullibility or complicity of distributors, off-premises retailers, and/or on-premises establishments. The role of e-commerce in distribution is, however, rapidly increasing, warranting attention as it facilitates sales expansion by illicit traders.

The presence of organised crime is also a particular concern in the illicit trade in alcohol, as actors of illicit trade exploit the price and taxation differentials between illicit and legitimate products. The substantial proceeds of illicit sales are used to fund other illegal activities, empowering criminal organisations while undermining the rule of law in counties.

The pandemic provided wide opportunities for illicit traders to adjust and expand their operations as government lockdowns, bans and other restrictions disrupted the alcohol market and created shortages. Overall, the pandemic gave impetus to the ongoing illicit trade in alcohol, creating more sophisticated international networks, logistics routes, and manufacturing techniques. The pandemic also highlighted the need for a global response based on enhanced co-operation among countries and greater collaboration with private sector stakeholders.

Beyond the market dynamics, illicit trade in alcohol has a wide range of negative socio-economic impacts. First, it poses significant health risks to consumers, when substandard products are manufactured using dangerous, unapproved ingredients. These negative impacts tend to disproportionally affect poorer and uneducated consumers.

In addition, illicit alcohol trade: i) deprives governments of tax revenues that would otherwise have been paid had the goods been sold in approved channels; ii) reduces sales by legitimate, tax-paying businesses and tarnishes their reputation when inferior, illicit products are sold under their brand; and iii) diverts resources to organised crime, which then uses the proceeds to sustain other illegal activities, undermining the rule of law.

Most countries have national alcohol policies, and issues dealing with illicit products are referenced in them, to various degrees. At an intergovernmental level, INTERPOL, Europol and the World Custom Organisation (WCO) have worked together on enforcement matters, conducting successful campaigns to disrupt illicit trade in alcohol. Industry stakeholders have also been working on this front, co-operating with governments and law enforcement around the world to develop solutions to tackle the illicit trade in a number of areas.

Abbreviations

ACEA	European Automobile Manufacturers Association
AACS	Alliance Against Counterfeit Spirits
B2C	Business to consumer
CEN	Customs Enforcement Network
CHAFEA	Consumers, Health, Agriculture and Food Executive Agency
FTZ	Free Trade Zones
HL	Hectolitres
IARD	International Alliance for Responsible Drinking
IAS	Institute of Alcohol Studies
IPR	Intellectual property rights
LEA	Law enforcement agency
NIH	National Institutes of Health
OCG	Organised criminal group
OLAF	European Anti-Fraud Office
RILO	Regional Intelligence Liaison Office
TF-CIT	OECD Task Force on Countering Illicit Trade
TRACIT	Transnational Alliance to Combat Illicit Trade
VAT	Value-added tax
WCO	World Customs Organization
WHO	World Health Organization
WTO	World Trade Organization
WWTG	World Wine Trade Group

1 Introduction

Illicit trade, which includes smuggled and counterfeit products as well as a number of other forms of unlawful trade, is a significant threat to society, businesses and consumers, undermining good governance, the rule of law and citizens' trust in government and legal businesses and trade. It has a negative impact on the sales and profits of legitimate firms and on the economy in general, while posing major health and safety threats to consumers.

The pandemic has exacerbated illicit trade and the negative impacts on economy and society. While communities and economies worldwide have been struggling with the health and economic effects of COVID-19, illicit trade has flourished, undermining people's health and safety when poor quality or toxic ingredients were used and increasing security risks with the rise of illegal activity. The trade has been facilitated by the Internet, via social media, e-commerce platforms, Free Trade Zones (FTZ), and online marketplaces, alarming law enforcement, and broader communities in many parts of the world.

Prior to the COVID-19 pandemic, global illicit trade was already booming through an array of trafficking and smuggling crimes. During the pandemic the situation changed, as governments introduced policies to stem the spread of the virus. Many countries, for example, imposed lockdowns which restricted the movement and activities of citizens, while illness curtailed production in many sectors, creating shortages in key goods. In the case of alcohol, some countries put limitations on the production and consumption of goods, keeping in mind the overall goal of protecting citizens' health. The restriction in the supply of alcohol products, however, fuelled illicit markets, which rose to meet unsatisfied demand, undermining the original intent and also with negative knock-on effects, including losses in tax revenues from alcohol sales and increased health and safety risks from impure and unsafe alcohol products.[1]

To address the problem of illicit trade in high risk sectors, the OECD Task Force on Countering Illicit Trade (TF-CIT) undertook a number of fact-finding exercises in recent years. These included a factual report on illicit trade in counterfeit pharmaceuticals (OECD/EUIPO, 2020[1]). It also included a series of webinars to discuss the impact of the pandemic on illicit trade in 2020 and 2021, with a view towards identifying the relevant governance gaps and market risks that should be addressed in further work on illicit trade. The webinars included sessions on:

- Illicit Trade in a Time of Crisis (April 2020)
- Trade in Fake Medicines at the Time of the Covid-19 Pandemics (June 2020);
- High-Risk Sectors in COVID Recovery (September 2020);
- Covid-19 Vaccine and the Threat of Illicit Trade (December 2020); and
- Crisis policy, illicit alcohol and lessons learned from lockdown (January 2021).

The webinars reveal that the key COVID-19-related elements that have affected the dynamics of illicit trade in high-risk sectors include the closure of borders, instances of restrictions on consumption, the reshaping of suppliers' structure and the destruction of existing relations in supply chains, as well as the change in enforcement priorities. The rapidity of changes in the market have made it difficult for countries to react in an effective manner, and corruption continues to fuel illicit trade worldwide.

This report has been prepared in further support of the work on high-risk sectors, focusing on alcohol. It follows up on the report on illicit trade in fake pharmaceuticals, and the set of workshop-specific reports.

This report: i) provides an overview of the alcohol industry, ii) examines the nature and scope of illicit trade in the sector, iii) assesses impacts that the illicit trade has had on economies, iv) identifies the factors driving illicit trade in the sector, v) reviews the measures that stakeholders have taken to better understand and combat the illicit trade, vi) examines the effects that measures taken by governments in light of the Covid-19 pandemic had on illicit trade, and vii) provides an overview of some of the key issues that need to addressed to deal with the societal challenges posed by illicit alcohol trade.

The analysis shows that the market for alcohol products is an attractive target for illicit trade and organised crime as the market is large, as are the profits that can be realised on the illicit trade, in some cases with little investment. The ease with which consumers can be deceived into buying counterfeit products, and the low risk of detection for all forms of illicit trade, create an irresistible cocktail for illicit traders, who continue to adapt their operations to elude law enforcement.

Reference

OECD/EUIPO (2020), *Trade in Counterfeit Pharmaceutical Products*, Illicit Trade, OECD Publishing, Paris, https://doi.org/10.1787/a7c7e054-en. [1]

Note

1 See: https://www.citizen.co.za/news/south-africa/3046546/liquor-ban-during-lockdown-exacerbated-alcohol-consumption/

2 Markets for alcohol

This chapter sets the scene by presenting the global alcohol industry: its main players, its international trade flows as well as its specificities in terms of marketing and distribution as in some countries the state plays an important regulatory role. It also clarifies what the illicit alcohol refers to and presents the specificities of this market

Industry structure

The world alcohol market is a trillion-dollar business, with revenues growing annually from USD 1.2 trillion in 2012, to USD 1.7 trillion in 2019.[1] With Covid-19-related lockdowns curtailing social and recreational activities, revenues eased to an estimated USD 1.5 and 1.4 trillion in 2020 and 2021, respectively. Growth is expected to resume, however, with revenues forecast to top USD 2.2 trillion in 2025.

The industry comprises three principal segments, with beer the largest (USD 552 billion in sales in 2021), followed by spirits (USD 468 billion) and wine (USD 306 billion), respectively.[2] The three segments account for over 90% of total sector sales.[3] The beer market is moderately concentrated, with the 10 largest companies accounting for over 70% of market share, while the 10 largest wine producers account for less than 15% of the market (Table 2.1).

Table 2.1. Largest alcoholic beverage companies, by volume and by segment, 2020

Segment/company	Headquarters	Market share (%)
Beer [1]		
Anheuser-Busch InBev	Belgium	30
Heineken	Netherlands	11
China Resources Snow Barrels	China	6
Molson Coors Brewing	United States	5
Carlsberg	Denmark	7
Tsingtao Brewing Company	China	5
Ashai	Japan	2
Beijing Yanjing Beer Group	China	3
Kirin	Japan	2
Constellation Brands	United States	1
Spirits[2]		
Diageo Plc	United Kingdom	9
Pernod Ricard SA	France	6
Hite Jinro	Korea	4
Shunxin	China	3
Thai Beverage	Thailand	3
Wine[3]		
EJ Gallo	Belgium	3
Constellation Brands	Unitod States	1.7
The Wine Group	United States	1.5
Treasury Wine Estate	Australia	1.2
Viña Conch Y Toro	Chile	1
Castel Frères	France	1
Accolade Wines	Australia	1
Pernod Ricard SA	France	<1
Grupo Penaflor	Argentina	<1
Fecovita Co-op	Argentina	<1

Notes: [1] See www.t4.ai/industry/beer-market-share.; [2] See (IAS, 2020[1]); [3] See www.zippia.com/advice/largest-wine-companies/.

Trade

International trade is an important source of revenue for the industry. In 2019, alcoholic beverages valued at USD 88.2 billion were traded across borders, which represented about 5% of production (Table 2.2). In the case of wine, about 10% of production was exported compared to 7% of spirits and 3% of beer. Wine and spirits each account for about 40% of total alcohol exports, whilst beer is about 20%. The degree to which products are exported depend in part on the tariffs imposed by countries on imports. These tariffs, which differ significantly among countries, averaged 24.3% in the case of wine, while they exceeded 30% in the case of spirits and beer. EU countries were the largest exporters in all product categories, with the United States a top exporter in 3 categories (spirits, beer and vermouth), and Mexico a large exporter of sprits and beer. Australia and Chile were top wine exporters, while Singapore and Japan were leading exporters of spirits and "other" fermented products (e.g. cider and rice wine), respectively.

Table 2.2. World exports of alcoholic beverages, 2019

(Billions of USD, except as noted)

Beverage	Exports	Average tariff	Leading export countries
Wine (HS 2204)	35.7	24.30%	France, Italy, Spain, Australia, Chile
Spirits (HS 2208)	33.9	30.90%	United Kingdom, France, Mexico, United States, Singapore
Beer (HS 2203)	16.5	32.70%	Mexico, Belgium, Netherlands, Germany, United States
Cider, etc. (HS 2206)	1.5	29%	Japan, Italy, Sweden, Canada, Germany
Vermouth (HS 2205)	0.6	30.40%	Italy, France, Spain, Germany, United States

Source: Observatory of Economic Complexity (https://oec.world/).

Marketing and distribution

The marketing and distribution of alcoholic beverages varies across countries, and can be complex, as governments play an important regulatory role. According to a 2018 WHO report, some 141 countries that took part in a WHO survey operated licensing systems for alcoholic beverages (86% of the total surveyed); about half (55%) had licensing at every level of the alcohol market (i.e. import, production, distribution, retail sales and export) (WHO, 2018[2]). Two additional countries reported subnational licensing for at least one level of the alcohol market.

Government supply and retail restrictions, often characterised as "monopolies", which can exist at all levels of the supply chain, were operational in a sizeable number of countries, with fifty countries reporting the use of such control at least one level. Monopolies involving imports (36 responding countries) and retail sales (35 countries) were most common for spirits, while monopolies for imports (33 responding countries), production (32 countries) and distribution (31 countries) were most common for beer. The number of reporting countries with a monopoly over exports (26) did not differ by beverage type. Of the countries with monopoly control over at least one level of the alcohol market, 19 (38%) had a monopoly at all levels.

Some countries employed a combination of licensing and monopoly systems, with 47 reporting a licensing system and a monopoly over at least one level of the market. It was, however, more common for countries to use licensing alone (94 countries). In some countries, such as the United States, controls at the state level were in addition to those imposed at the federal level (Box 2.1).

Box 2.1. Regulation of US market for alcoholic beverages

In the United States, a unique three-tier system governing the distribution and sale of alcoholic beverages is in place.[1] Manufacturers (tier 1) sell to licensed wholesalers, distributors or control boards (tier 2), which, in turn, sell to licensed outlets (such as bars, restaurants and liquor stores) (tier 3). Federal excise taxes are collected from the manufacturer when goods change hands, or, in the case of imported goods, from the importer when products exit bonded facilities.[2] Distributors and control boards act in co-operation with the federal and state governments to help ensure that taxes are collected. Tier[3] entities ensure that parties purchasing the beverages are of legal age. The system is not, however, totally closed, as some manufacturers are able to sell at least some of their production directly to consumers, either on their premises or through mail, Internet or telephone orders. Supporters of the three-tier system note that it provides a number of important benefits, including: i) regulatory benefits, by helping to ensure that laws and regulations governing the distribution of products are followed; ii) economic benefits, by helping to ensure that taxes are faithfully collected; and iii) public health benefits, by lowering the risk that counterfeit or tainted products are introduced into the supply chain.

Notes: 1 See www.nabca.org/three-tier-system-modern-view-0; 2.See www.parkstreet.com/wine-spirits-industry-background/; 3 See www.nabca.org/three-tier-system-modern-view-0.

Licit and illicit products

Before turning to the analysis of illicit trade in alcohol, it is important to clarify what distinguishes licit alcohol from illicit alcohol, and how the markets for alcohol are structured.

"Licit" alcohol includes those products that are manufactured and adhere to regulatory requirements and are subsequently recorded and distributed in an approved manner, and two types of products that are not recorded: i) informal alcohol, which are beverages that may be sometimes produced legally outside of formal production channels and whose production and consumption tend to follow cultural and artisanal practices and ii) licit items which consumers legally transport from one jurisdiction to another, for their personal use, such as duty-free.

"Illicit" items, on the other hand, may not be produced according to regulations and standards, may be produced and traded outside of legal channels, or they may be legally produced in one jurisdiction but traded outside of the formal alcohol market in another. As a result they are not officially recorded and evade tax, excise, customs or intellectual property legislation (Skehan, Sanchez and Hastings, 2016[3]). Illicit products, which are not recorded, include those i) on which taxes might not be paid, ii) which might not be fit for human consumption, or iii) which might otherwise undermine legitimate business and trade.

Examples of illicit trade include:

- Contraband or smuggled alcohol, which are products with original branding that have been illegally imported or smuggled into a jurisdiction and sold without payment of tariffs or excise taxes,
- Counterfeit alcohol, which are fraudulent imitations of legitimate branded products that violate the intellectual property rights (IPR) of legitimate producers (see Box 2.2).
- Products that are not produced in accordance with legal requirements and may therefore pose health risks,
- Products sold with false or misleading packaging (including the sale of alcohol in bottles which have been refilled with substitute products).

- "Third shift" alcohol, which are genuine products produced clandestinely at licensed facilities (and are not properly recorded)
- Surrogate alcohol, which are products that are legally produced for other purposes and not intended for human consumption, but are nonetheless imbibed (such as hand sanitizer, mouthwash, aftershave or cologne, rubbing alcohol, windshield washer fluid or an antifreeze).

Box 2.2. Counterfeit alcohol

Counterfeit alcohol is alcohol that is deliberately and fraudulently mislabeled as a registered trademark. Importantly, such counterfeiting refers only to a registered trademark, and does not included a large volume of mislabelled illicit alcohol that might still deceive consumers (and pose their health at risk) but does not infringe any trademark. For example a bottle of an unbranded, substandard alcoholic beverage offered on illicit markets with a label "vodka" is clearly illicit, yet it might not infringe any trademark, hence not be counterfeit.

The market for alcohol (licit and illicit) is also characterised by the manner in which is treated officially, namely whether the production is recorded or unrecorded:

- The recorded alcohol market segment includes legally produced and traded beverages that are reflected in official statistics and are subject to regulation. Most commercially and legally traded branded beverages are recorded.
- The unrecorded alcohol market segment, by definition, is not reflected in official statistics and is not subject to the same regulations as the recorded market. Some unrecorded products are licit, but, for various reasons, escape being captured in records. Such products include alcohol purchased through legal cross-border shopping for beverages recorded in the country of purchase but not in the country of consumption, and legal informal alcohol, which is licit but not recorded. It also includes 'surrogate' alcohol, legally produced for other purposes, often not potable, yet consumed.

E-commerce

E-commerce has boomed across many countries, far exceeding overall growth in traditional retail sales. Overall, sales of goods and services by businesses to consumers (B2C) over the Internet increased by 82% worldwide between 2016 to 2019, with a Covid-19-associated boost of 25.7% in 2020, to USD 4.2 trillion.[4] By 2025, e-commerce retail sales are currently forecast to rise to USD 7.2 trillion, which would represent about 24.5% of total retail sales, as compared to 17.8% in 2020. Alcoholic beverages demonstrated particularly high growth in online sales during the pandemic and are expected to continue to accelerate in the future, at growth rates greater than e-commerce in general. After growing by 11% in 2019, a November 2020 assessment forecast that the value of alcohol e-commerce would increase by 42% in 2020, across 10 core markets, to reach USD 24 billion.[5] By 2024, e-commerce sales in these 10 markets, plus an additional 10 "markets to watch" were expected to grow to USD necessity 40 billion.[6]

While the increase in online sales, including online sales of alcohol, has been attributed in large part to consumer responses to lockdowns, it is expected that interest in online purchasing will strengthen as brand owners increasingly invest in the channel. In the United States, online "off-trade" sales,[7] which increased by 80% in 2020 alone (albeit from a low base), are expected to grow by six-fold from 2019 to 2024, increasing market share from 1% to 7%. Increased awareness by consumers of the availability of alcohol online, combined with relaxation of regulations in some jurisdictions to facilitate online sales and home deliveries are also factors supporting the e-commerce growth.[8] Some 44% of alcohol e-shoppers, for example, only started buying alcohol online in 2020. The growth in e-commerce sales contrasts with the overall market for alcoholic beverage, which dipped in 2020 and is not expected to reach pre-Covid levels until 2023 (IWSR, 2021).

Another factor fuelling growth in e-commerce sales is the growing number of business entities establishing an Internet e-commerce presence. As a matter of survival in the face of massively decreased "on-trade" sales in, for example, restaurants closed during the pandemic, smaller wineries in the United States, and likely elsewhere, developed websites to promote sales of their products in response to the pandemic (Guynn, 2020[4]). In support of their online endeavours, they also utilised YouTube and Instagram Live to promote sales, while using Facebook and Goggle ads to expand their customer bases and attract customers. At the same time, sales sharply rose at retail wine sites early on in the pandemic, and through mobile shipping apps like Drizly, Doordash and Instacart. At Wine.com, revenue quadrupled to more than USD 1 million a day in the early months, with the retailer responding by hiring 500 people and tripling its marketing spend.

Before the pandemic, the extent to which illicit alcohol has been sold on the Internet has been limited, reflecting the strict controls over production and distribution of alcohol in general, at least in the more highly regulated markets. With the loosening of regulations during COVID-19 and the active development of Internet sales by producers and retailers, however, opportunities for trafficking in illicit products will likely become more attractive for counterfeiters. Examples of e-commerce fraud for wine and whiskey has emerged in a number of markets, including the well-regulated US marketplace (Box 2.3). The cases are illustrative of the nature of e-commerce fraud; establishing the overall scope of misuse of the Internet to facilitate illegal sales of illicit alcoholic beverages is unknown, but one can presume the scale could be significant and growing.

While public and private stakeholders have taken many actions to combat illicit trade in e-commerce, significant challenges remain, as criminal networks have been able to react quickly and dynamically to avoid detection and circumvent law enforcement. In response, governments and industry are constantly examining their policies to mitigate illicit trade online. As identified in (OECD/EUIPO, 2021b[5]) there are several areas that need to be addressed in this regard. This includes such issues as the difficulties in dealing with a vast landscape that includes millions of sellers, or enforcement gaps and limited institutional capacities exploited by counterfeiters and criminal networks. It also includes issues related to adequately screening cross-border movements of counterfeits, many of which are shipped in small parcels and letter packets.

Box 2.3. Examples of illicit trade in alcohol on-line

In China, one Internet merchant selling a range of premium champagne products on Tmall, a site operated by Alibaba, was found in 2019 to have been selling counterfeit Dom Perignon Luminous Millesime Brut 2002 champagne. [1] Moët Hennessy, the brand owner, uncovered the fraud after buying and inspecting two cases of the champagne. The company found that the product had inconsistencies in wine label design, font size, vintage discrepancy between label and cork, shoddy typos on its back labels, and false use of luminous labels. The extent of the fraud could not be definitively established. The company, which paid RMB 43 000 for the two cases, sought relief in a court case, and was eventually awarded RMB 80 000, which was one-third the RMB 500 000 requested. In making the award, the court noted that information supplied by the Internet platform suggested that limited quantities of fake products had been sold; it also noted that because the scale of the fraudster's fake wine operation could not be determined, there was no evidence to prove the loss to Moët Hennessy.

In Italy, authorities working with Europol disrupted a major fraudulent operation in 2018, in which empty bottles of high-quality wines were refilled with low quality beverages and marketed on a large e-commerce platform as genuine ones that were "on sale".[2] The wines were sold globally in Belgium, France, Germany, Italy, Spain and the United States.

In the United States, Buffalo Trace Distillery, which produces high-end bourbon has been subject to a number of online counterfeiting scams. In 2017, the company launched a USD 500 000 campaign to fight against online counterfeiting, which ended up with the conviction of at least one counterfeiter of the high-priced bourbon.[3] In 2021, the company issued a public warning to customers over an increasing number of fraudulent and counterfeit whiskeys being sold online. Some customers complained that they had never received their order; others received bottles that used plastic toppers rather than the metal toppers used on the genuine product.[4] Despite taking legal actions to have offending sites shut down and sending notices to social media companies, the situation continued to be of concern. The counterfeiters were effectively evading the ban in most US jurisdictions against shipping alcohol directly to consumers. The majority of the scams, it was noted, involved foreign websites.

In the United Kingdom, a whiskey auction site discovered suspicious bottles during routine authenticity checks in 2017[5]. Enforcement authorities visited the seller's home where they discovered a counterfeiting operation with a scale of sophistication purportedly never before seen in spirits. Alongside a genuine collection was a large-scale fraudulent set-up where hundreds of old bottles were being refilled with cheaper, younger liquids.

Notes:
1 See https://vino-joy.com/2021/06/30/moet-hennessy-lures-out-fake-dom-perignon-fraudster-in-china/
and https://mp.weixin.qq.com/s/yVM6NUmHQXoZCqi5mrdHLQ.
2 See www.europol.europa.eu/newsroom/news/fake-wines-sold-under-expensive-italian-labels-market.
3 See www.thespiritsbusiness.com/2017/10/buffalo-trace-battles-fake-pappy-with-us500k-investment/.
4 See www.thedrinksbusiness.com/2021/09/buffalo-trace-warns-of-increasing-number-of-counterfeit-whiskies-being-sold-online/.
5 See www.thespiritsbusiness.com/2017/03/whisky-auction-site-uncovers-fake-booze-plot/.

References

Guynn, J. (2020), *"Coronavirus wine: Wineries turn to online sales to avoid getting crushed by the COVID-19 pandemic"*, USA Today, May 27, https://eu.usatoday.com/story/tech/2020/05/27/wine-sales-move-online-coronavirus-quarantine-wine-delivery/5241525002/. [4]

IAS (2020), *The alcohol industry: An overview*, Institute of Alcohol Studies, http://www.ias.org.uk/wp-content/uploads/2020/12/The-alcohol-industry-%E2%80%93-An-overview.pdf. [1]

OECD/EUIPO (2021b), *Global Trade in Fakes: a Worrying Threat*, OECD Publishing, https://www.oecd.org/publications/global-trade-in-fakes-74c81154-en.htm. [5]

Skehan, P., I. Sanchez and L. Hastings (2016), "The size, impacts and drivers of illicit trade in alcohol", in *Illicit Trade: Converging Criminal Networks*, OECD Publishing, Paris, https://doi.org/10.1787/9789264251847-10-en. [3]

WHO (2018), *Global status report on alcohol and health*, World Health Organization, Geneva, https://apps.who.int/iris/rest/bitstreams/1151838/retrieve. [2]

Notes

[1] See www.statista.com/forecasts/696641/market-value-alcoholic-beverages-worldwide.

[2] See www.statista.com/forecasts/696641/market-value-alcoholic-beverages-worldwide.

[3] Hard seltzer, cider, perry and rice wine account for the remaining 10%.

[4] See www.statista.com/statistics/379046/worldwide-retail-e-commerce-sales/ and www.emarketer.com/content/global-ecommerce-forecast-2021.

[5] The 10 core markets (Australia, Brazil, China, France, Germany, Italy, Japan, Spain, United Kingdom and the United States) account for about 90% of total e-commerce sales.

[6] The "markets to watch" are Mexico, Colombia, Argentina, Netherlands, Israel, Nigeria, Kenya, South Africa, Singapore.

[7] Sales to retail outlets, as opposed "on-trade" sales to restaurants, bars, etc.

[8] The relaxation in restrictions in online sales were in some instances introduced as temporary measures.

3 Illicit trade in alcohol – what we know so far?

This chapter analyses the illicit alcohol market in depth. In addition to provide general information on the scale and magnitude of the market, it identifies the main drivers of this market, whose profitability is particularly high due to the specific taxation (excise tax) of alcohol. It also analyses the role of organised crime in this market as well as elements related to the penalties incurred. Finally, it addresses a specific aspect of the illicit alcohol market by focusing on counterfeit alcohol.

Scale and magnitude

The magnitude and scope of illicit trade in alcoholic beverages are vast. According to the WHO, unrecorded consumption of alcohol, much of which is presumed to be illicit, accounted for 25% of total world consumption in 2016 (WHO, 2018[1]). The share, however, varied significantly among regions and countries, ranging from 14% in the case of the Americas, to 67% in the eastern Mediterranean region (Table 3.1). Income levels are also an important determinant; in high income countries, the average share of unrecorded alcohol consumed was 11.4% in 2016, compared to 37% and 44% in lower income and lower middle-income countries. The higher percentages in the lower income countries are likely to reflect the interest consumers may have in seeking out lower priced alternatives to licit products or to circumvent restrictions on availability of legal alcohol, as well as the ability of illicit traders to penetrate distribution channels more easily. The WHO expects the share of unrecorded alcohol globally to continue to rise, to an estimated 27.7% of consumption in 2025.

Table 3.1 Per capita consumption of alcohol and share that is unrecorded, by region, 2016

Region	Per capita consumption (litres)	Share of consumption that is unrecorded (%)
Africa	6.3	32
America	8	14
Eastern Mediterranean	0.6	67
Europe	9.8	18
Southeast Asia	4.5	47
Western Pacific	7.3	21
World	6.4	25

Source: (WHO, 2018[1]).

A regional study of illicit alcohol in 24 Latin American, African and Eastern European countries provides further insights into the scope of the market (Euromonitor International, 2018[2]). The study estimated that 25.8% of the 42.3 million hectolitres of alcohol consumed each year across the countries (in alcohol equivalents) was illicit, providing illicit merchants with USD 19.4 billion in black market revenue. While all alcoholic beverages are subject to illicit trade, the study revealed that the degree of illicit trade varies by product. Beer, for example represented 52.9% of total recorded consumption of alcoholic beverages, (in terms of alcohol equivalents), but only about 10% of total illicit trade, meaning that illicit beer was actually just 2.3% of total alcohol consumption. (Euromonitor International, 2018[2]). According to the report, overall, the bulk of the illicit trade problem was in higher value distilled spirits, which accounted for 81% of illicit trade in alcohol. Wine and other products, at ~9%, accounted for the balance.

The study also examined the relative importance of the types of illicit trade in the countries studied, finding that the greatest volume of illicit trade was tied to the non-payment of taxes within jurisdictions, followed by counterfeiting, illicit trade in artisanal products, and smuggling (Table 3.2). Of further note, there is also often an aspirational component to illicit purchases. Since illicit alcoholic beverages have lower prices than their licit counterparts, consumers are able to afford premium products (or what they believe to be legitimate premium products) that would otherwise be unaffordable. The desire to gain access to products consumed by people of higher socioeconomic status is common across countries, and affects a wide range of illicit products, including alcohol. (Euromonitor International, 2018[2]).

Table 3.2. Relative importance of different types of illicit trade

Percent of total hectoliters of illicit trade

Illicit practice	Share of illicit trade (%)	Description
Tax leakage	30	Alcoholic beverages legally manufactured in the country, but for which required taxes have not been paid.
Counterfeit and unregistered brands	24	This category includes both fraudulent imitations of branded beverages as well as industrially manufactured beverages that are either unbranded or sold under unregistered brands.
Illicit artisanal products	22	Alcoholic beverages produced following artisanal practices, including home production. Artisanal alcoholic beverages are considered illicit if they are produced for commercial purposes and if their production and/or sale violate local law.
Smuggling	17	Smuggling (also known as contraband) covers both ethanol, which can be used as a raw ingredient for spirits production), as well as finished products that have been brought into a country for commercial purposes without paying required import tariffs duties, and fees.
Surrogate	7	Alcohol not meant for human consumption but diverted to the market for alcoholic beverages. Examples include pharmaceutical alcohol, mouthwash, and perfume.

Source: (Euromonitor International, 2018[2])

Further insights into the scope of illicit trade are provided by the WCO, which issues an annual report on illicit trade, with special attention to the situation in alcoholic beverages. In its 2020 report, the WCO notes that, in general, governments are increasingly facing well-networked and organised traffickers whose smuggling activities are harder to detect and disrupt as smugglers continuously develop more sophisticated techniques to thwart law enforcement (WCO, 2020[3]). With respect to alcohol, customs authorities reported 5,326 seizures of alcoholic products, totaling 1.9 million liters of beverages in 2019, which was down by 44% and 63%, respectively, from their 2018 levels (WCO, 2020[3]).[1] The Middle East, Western Europe and Eastern and Central Europe accounted for much of the reported seizures. On a country level, Saudi Arabia and Ireland together reported 71% of all cases in 2019, with the top 15 reporting countries together accounting for 96% of the total. With respect to detection methods for alcohol and related areas (such as tobacco), customs reported that 56% of cases were the result of routine investigations, 38% reflected risk profiling, 3% resulted from intelligence-led investigations, and 2% were generated from random checks.

The predominant means of conveyance were i) by vehicles, which accounted for 67% of total seizures (65% of the total number of liters seized), and ii) by air (11% and 1%, respectively). Pedestrian seizures, on the other hand, while accounting for only 3% of total seizures, accounted for 14% of the total volume seized. Much of the illicit trade (74%) was regionally based.

Drivers of illicit trade in alcohol

The magnitude and scope of illicit trade in alcoholic beverages is linked to a number of drivers, including the profitability of illicit operations linked to the price differential between licit and illicit alcohol products, the degree to which legitimate markets can be penetrated with illicit products, the risk of illicit traders being caught by law enforcement, and the severity of the penalties that are, or could be, imposed. As discussed earlier the illicit market includes trade in both genuine, illegally produced and counterfeit products that are smuggled across borders. This section examines the profitability and viability of smuggling operations involving all illicit products, along with the penalties for parties which engage in the smuggling. Further attention is then paid to the market for counterfeit and illegally produced alcohol, which offers illicit traders with additional opportunities to exploit consumers.

Profitability

The principal factor driving illicit sales in alcoholic beverages is price differential between illicit and licit alcohol that is linked directly to the difference in taxes and tariffs imposed on various alcoholic products across countries. These include differences in i) value-added taxes (VAT) and related sales taxes, which are imposed by many countries on most goods, ii) customs tariffs, and iii) excise taxes, which are imposed on selected products, including alcohol, to generate revenue and/or discourage consumption. Significant differences exist between countries in the rates applied to various alcohol beverages, providing an incentive for illicit cross-border trade (e.g., smuggling). However, there are also significant differences in fiscal policies applied to different beverage types within individual countries.

These differentials -be they at country or category level- create demand for cheaper products. This demand is filled by illicit alcohol and also explains why spirits comprise a significant proportion of global illicit alcohol (Euromonitor, 2018a). Consumers unable to afford legal spirits brands are left with two options — less expensive alternatives, or to turn to the illicit market.

As shown in Table 3.3, the economic incentive to traffic alcohol based on tax differentials is high. In the case of beer, scotch and gin, the differentials in excise taxes in the OECD area are more than 40%, making these products particularly attractive for traffickers, but there are also incentives for trafficking low-priced wines, where the differential exceeds 50%. Differences in VAT and related sales taxes can provide further incentives for trafficking. In the European Union, for example, VAT rates, as of 1 January 2021, ranged from 17% in the case of Luxembourg to 27% in the case of Hungary. Globally, some countries have no VAT or related sales taxes, while taxes in others, such as the United States, are imposed at the sub-federal level (OECD, 2020[4]). Further incentives may arise if customs tariffs are significant. As shown in Table 3.4, such tariffs are generally low in the OECD countries listed, but are significantly higher in the case of Brazil, where duties are 20% in most product categories, and India, where tariffs are 150% in most categories.

Table 3.3. VAT and excise tax rates on selected alcoholic beverages, in selected OECD countries

(Percent of sale prices for high- and low-priced products)

Country	VAT and related federal sales taxes	Excise taxes				
		Beer	Wine	Cognac	Gin	Scotch
		Percent of sale prices for high- and low-priced products				
Australia	10	19-35	(1)	24-26	57-62	56-63
France	20	5-10	0-2	13-16	35-42	27-32
Germany	19	4-7	3-20	11-14	26-31	20-25
Italy	22	10-16	(1)	14-15	27-34	21-22
Japan	10	29-42	1-6	(1)	(1)	(1)
United Kingdom	20	22-39	5-36	25-31	44-52	32-40
United States	0	23-28	1-8	7-8	16-19	11-13
Lowest tax in OECD	0	4-5	0-2	5-5	16-19	11-13
Highest tax in OECD	27	51-59	15-53	38-41	60-67	56-63

Note: (1) Not available.
Source: (Ngo Anh P. et al., 2021[5]) and (OECD, 2020[4])

Table 3.4. WTO MFN applied duty rates on alcoholic beverages[1]

(ad valorem, except as noted)

Country	Beer (HS 2203)	Wine (HS 2204)	Vermouth -2205	Cider, etc. (HS 2206)	Spirits (HS 2208)
Australia	0%	5%	5%	0% to 5%	5%
Brazil	20%	20%	20%	20%	12%-20%
Canada	0%	0% to CAD .0468/l	0%	3%, or	0%, or
				CAD 0.0211 to 0.2816/l, or	CAD 0.0492 to 0.2456/l of absolute ethanol, or
				CAD 0.1228/l of absolute ethanol	CAD 0.352/l
China	0%	14% to 30%	65%	40%	10%
European Union	0	32% or	EUR 9 to 10.9/hl, or	EUR 5.76 to 19.2/hl, or	0%, or
		EUR 12.1 to 32/hl, or	EUR 0.9/% vol/hl to EUR 0.9/% vol/hl + EUR 6.4/hl	EUR 1.3/% vol/hl (min EUR 7.2/hl)	EUR 0.6/% vol/hl to EUR 0.6/% vol/hl+ EUR 3.2/hl, or
		Other			EUR 1/% vol/hl to EUR 1/% vol/hl + EUR 6.4/hl
India	100%	150%	150%	150%	150%
Japan	0%	19.1% to 25.5%, or	19.1%, or	JPY 27 to 70.4/l, or	0% to 18%, or
		JPY 45 to 182/liter, or	JPY 69.3/l	Greater of 29.8% or JPY 23/kg	JPY 70.4 to 126/l, or
		Lesser of 15%, or JPY 125/l, but not less than JPY 67/l, or			Lesser of 17.5% or JPY 77/l
		Greater of 29.8% or JPY 23.8/kg			
United Kingdom	0%	0% to 40%, or	0%	GBP 4.84 to 16/hl, or	0%, or
		GBP 10 to 26/hl		GBP 1/% vol/hl	GBP 0.5/% vol/hl to GBP 0.5/% vol/hl + GBP 2.6/hl, or
					GBP 0.8/%vol/hl to GBP 0.8/% vol/hl + GBP 5.3/hl
United States	0%	USD 0.053 to 22.4/l, or	USD 0.035 to 0.042/l	USD 0.004/l, or	0%, or
		USD 0.044/l + USD 0.314/pf. l		USD 0.031/l + USD 0.221/pf. l on ethyl alcohol content, or	USD 0.0211 to 0.237/pf. l
				USD 0.03-0.139/l	

Notes: 1 Within each 4-digit HS category there are often numerous line items with different tariff levels. Some are expressed on an ad valorem basis, while others are specific rates that are applied on various bases. Where tariffs are expressed on comparable bases, ranges are shown; Abbreviations: l = litre; hl = hectolitre; % vol = alcohol percentage ; pf. = proof ; kg = kilogramme
Source: WTO, http://tao.wto.org/report/TariffLines.aspx.

Marketing illicit alcohol

Trafficking products from low-taxed areas to higher priced ones is highly profitable, as little or no investment is required to engage in the trafficking, which can be carried on a small scale periodically by individuals, or on a large scale by organised criminal networks. One of the main attractions of the illicit trafficking is that the products involved can be genuine, thereby requiring no tampering. The sole risk for the traffickers is shipments being discovered and intercepted by law enforcement while in transit. The risk is likely to be low, as much of the illicit trade is carried out by road transport; the challenges for enforcement to intercept the shipments are significant as in the European Union alone there were more than 6.2 million commercial trucks in use in 2019 (ACEA, 2021[6]).

Infiltrating established supply chains, however, may be challenging, as the sale and serving of alcohol are regulated activities, often requiring parties to obtain licenses to engage in the activities. As discussed earlier, in some cases, states exercise monopoly control over retail sales, further restricting distribution channels. The ability of counterfeiters to penetrate markets is thus limited, only thriving when distributors, retailers and/or establishments serving alcohol are complicit in the marketing of the counterfeit products.

The increased use of the Internet by producers (of wine in particular) and retailers to promote alcohol sales also has implications for illicit traders, as clever marketing and low prices could provide a means for them to expand markets.

Role of organised crime

The profitability of trade in illicit alcohol has attracted the attention of organised crime, which is a major player in the market. A case study of five EU countries (Greece, Italy, Poland, Romania and Spain) confirmed that Organized Criminal Groups (OCGs) dominate the illicit trade in tobacco, alcohol and pharmaceuticals (Ellis, 2017[7]). While some small-scale activity may exist, the study found that the role of OCGs in co-ordinating, conducting and ultimately profiting from large-scale activity in illicit trade was repeatedly highlighted in interviews with authorities in the countries concerned, in official documents and by existing research. The evolution of OCGs to loose, undefined and flexible networks was seen as increasing their effectiveness by promoting co-operation, in producing illicit products, obtaining false documentation, and exploiting EU tax regulations (Box 3.1). As discussed later in the report, enforcement authorities have been actively engaged in disrupting OCGs engaged in illicit alcohol trade in recent years.

Box 3.1. Example of OCG tax fraud in alcohol scheme

In 2014, joint action by eight member states, supported by Eurojust and Europol, targeted multiple OCGs that had been involved in a sophisticated carousel fraud scheme. The groups were using falsified export documents to create a complex supply chain across EU member states, including duplicated and phantom transactions. Their intention was to conceal the destination of the alcohol being traded, thereby avoiding the payment of VAT. Nineteen members of the OCGs were arrested in Germany, Italy Romania and the United Kingdom. In total, 31 premises were searched, leading to the seizure of financial assets, weapons, computers, vehicles, mobile phones and documents.

Sources: (Ellis, 2017[7]) and www.europol.europa.eu/newsroom/news/europol-and-eurojust-support-successful-action-against-alcohol-carousel-fraud .

Legal frameworks

Smuggling and tax evasion can carry stiff penalties, but they are not a sufficient deterrent as illicit trade in alcohol continues to thrive, and at times involve authorities themselves. More attention is needed to enforce laws and impose sanctions and penalties at levels sufficient to deter illegal activity. The penalties include confiscation of the smuggled merchandise (although not always obligation to destroy), fines and imprisonment. Moreover, imposing administrative, criminal and civil penalties for illicit trade in alcohol could prohibit illicit traders from exploiting markets with the weakest penal regimes.[2]

Effective enforcement requires co-ordination between countries countries (to prevent counterfeiting or smuggling), between different national government agencies (to align fiscal, health and security priorities) and between different levels of government (federal, state, and municipal to ensure consistency and to mitigate potential corruption). Corruption, complicity, and collusion can hinder collaboration and starve governments of the internal will to enforce policies. Bribery is particularly common, and it can occur in all parts of the supply chain.

Table 3.5 below summarises the magnitude and scope of penalties for smuggling and tax evasion in a number of countries around the world.

Table 3.5. Criminal sanctions and fines for alcohol smuggling and related tax evasion

Country	Note
Australia	Fiscal fraud is subject to imprisonment of up to 10 years under the country's Criminal Code. In addition, under the Customs Act, smuggling is subject to a fine of up to 5 times the amount of the duty due, or, if the amount if duty due is unknown, up to AUD 222 000 (1 000 penalty units); the goods in question are, moreover, forfeited.
Brazil	Under the country's Penal Code, smuggling of goods is generally subject to imprisonment ranging from one to four years.
Canada	Under the country's Customs Act, minor cases of smuggling are subject to a fine of not more than CAD 50 000, or to imprisonment for a term not exceeding six months or to both. An indicted smuggler, however, is to a fine of not more than CAD 500 000, or to imprisonment for a term not exceeding five years, or to both. In both cases, the smuggled merchandise is subject to seizure; in the case of wine and spirits, such seizures are permanent.
China	Smuggling goods and articles carrying a tax of over CNY 500 000 are punishable with imprisonment of over 10 years or life imprisonment, with a fine of over 100 percent but less than 500 percent of the evaded taxes, or forfeiture of property. Offenses of an extraordinary serious nature, however, are punishable with life imprisonment or death, with forfeiture of property.
	Smuggling goods and articles carrying a tax over CNY 150 000 yuan but less than CNY 500 000 yuan are punishable with imprisonment of over three years but less than 10 years, with a fine of over 100 percent but less than 500 percent of the evaded taxes. Offenses of an extraordinarily serious nature are punishable with imprisonment of over 10 years or life imprisonment, with a fine of over 100 percent but less than 500 percent of the evaded taxes, or forfeiture of property.
	Smuggling goods and articles carrying a tax over 50 000 yuan and less than 150 000 yuan are punishable with imprisonment or criminal detention of less than three years, with a fine of over 100 percent and less than 500 percent of the evaded taxes.
United Kingdom	Lesser offences are generally subject to fines, but imprisonment can occur via custodial sentences of up to 6 months. If a smuggler is indicted, however, prison terms could stretch to 5 to 7 years. Moreover, in cases involving the smuggling of prohibited goods or the illegal manufacture of excise goods, maximum imprisonment could stretch to 14 years, depending on the nature of the goods. With respect to fines, the level imposed could be up to 100% of the tax loss, or, where there is a lack of co-operation or disclosure, up to 200% of the tax loss. In the case of VAT fraud, fines of up to 70% of the amount owed could be imposed; moreover, in extreme cases, parties could face sentences of up to life imprisonment.
United States	In the United States, smuggling goods results in the merchandise being seized; parties involved in the smuggling are subject to imprisonment of up to 20 years, and/or a fine. Moreover, evading excise taxes on beer or wine can result in a fine of up to USD 5 000 and/or imprisonment of up to 5 years, or both, for each offence; in addition, all the product and equipment use in the production of the beer and wine made will be forfeited. For spirits, the penalties for tax evasion are up to USD 10 000 and/or up to 5 years in prison. Wilful attempts to evade or defeat any Internal Revenue Code tax, however, are subject to fines of up to USD 100 000 and/or 5 years in prison,

Sources : Brazil: www.loc.gov/item/global-legal-monitor/2014-07-03/brazil-penal-code-amended/; Canada: https://laws-lois.justice.gc.ca/eng/acts/C-52.6/page-39.html#docCont and https://laws-lois.justice.gc.ca/eng/acts/c-52.6/page-33.html#h-141688; China: www.fmprc.gov.cn/ce/cgvienna/eng/dbtyw/jdwt/crimelaw/t209043.htm; United Kingdom: www.dbtandpartners.co.uk/specialisms/tax-services/smuggling/, https://admiraltax.co.uk/penalties-for-uk-tax-fraud-explained/ and www.dbtandpartners.co.uk/specialisms/tax-services/vat-repayment-fraud/; United States: www.law.cornell.edu/uscode/text/26/5671, www.law.cornell.edu/uscode/text/26/5661, /www.law.cornell.edu/uscode/text/26/5602, and. www.law.cornell.edu/uscode/text/26/7201.

The approach that governments take when governing the production and sale of alcohol can leave the door open for the illicit alcohol market, unintentionally stimulating it. This is particularly the case when the governance frameworks do not assure effective co-ordination and information sharing between government agencies and the public, private and civil society sectors.

This was particularly striking during the COVID-19 pandemic, when supply chains were disrupted and many traditional outlets, such as bars and restaurants, were closed. At the same time existing trade routes were also changing rapidly posing a challenge to enforcement that also suffered from labor shortages. Illicit traders leveraged this opportunity by broadened the range of their activities, in some instances manufacturing the entire product, using fake bottles, rather than collecting used, genuine ones. This enabled them to greatly accelerate their "time to market", making it possible to have a dramatic impact in a very short time in markets worldwide. [3]

A review of UK experiences reveals smuggling continues to be significant. During 2016-20, the total number of instances of cross-border smuggling of alcoholic beverages in the United Kingdom increased, surging in 2019 and 2020, to levels far exceeding their 2016 and 2017 levels (Table 3.6). Most of the surge occurred in beer, which accounted for 75% of the total volume of smuggled products. Customs seized only a small fraction of the products, with most instances referred to the UK's tax authorities for further action. The spike is in contrast to inland seizures of smuggled products, the volume of which fell by more than one half, with an even sharper decline in 2021, when Covid restrictions were at a high level (Table 3.7). The downward trend occurred in all categories, except that in 2021, seizures of spirits rose to a period high. With respect to criminal sanctions, the number of arrests and convictions during 2016/17 to 2020/21 totaled 45 and 28, respectively (Table 3.8).

Table 3.6. UK tax revenues protected through detection of unpaid excise duty on spirits, beer and wine at the UK border, 2016-2020

Product	2016	2017	2018	2019	2020 (9 months)
Total, seized products and products referred to HM Revenue & Customs for further checks					
Volume (1 000 litres)					
Spirits	1 261	1 577	1 395	2 996	1 999
Beer	28 429	24 657	17 390	44 200	42 118
Wine	7 107	8 763	3 900	12 569	12 370
Total	36 797	34 997	22 685	59 765	56 487
Value (1,000 GBP)					
Spirits	16 231	17 979	15 130	32 417	21 493
Beer	26 364	20 497	13 660	34 341	32 244
Wine	23 240	26 473	11 042	36 692	35 771
Total	65 835	64 949	39 832	103 450	89 508
Seized products					
Liters (1,000):					
Spirits	na	na	81	146	46
Beer	na	na	2 104	3 940	1 232
Wine	na	na	344	1 177	553
Total	na	na	2 529	5 263	1 831
Value (1,000 GBP)					
Spirits	na	na	1 078	1 953	612
Beer	na	na	2 005	3 743	1 170
Wine	na	na	1 190	4 195	1 974
Total	na	na	4 273	9 891	3 756

Note: na: Not available

Source: See www.gov.uk/government/publications/border-force-transparency-data-q2-2021

Table 3.7. UK inland seizures of beer, spirits and wine, 2016-2021

Product	Apr 2016-Mar 2017	Apr 2017-Mar 2018	Apr 2018-Mar 2019	Apr 2019-Mar 2020	Apr 2020-Mar 2021
Volume (1,000 litres)					
Beer	1 875	1 473	1 214	845	103
Spirits	170	64	50	41	174
Wine	373	376	356	262	11
Total	2 417	1 912	1 620	1 148	288
Duty (1,000 GBP)					
Beer	1 744	1 414	1 153	803	98
Spirits	2 182	851	672	549	2 327
Wine	1 242	1 299	1 232	936	40
Total	5 157	3 565	3 057	2 288	2 465

Note: Totals based on unrounded data.
Source: See https://www.gov.uk/government/publications/tackling-alcohol-smuggling-outputs.

Table 3.8. Criminal enforcement involving inward smuggling of alcohol in the United Kingdom, 2016-21

Period (Apr-Mar)	Number of arrests	Number of convictions
2016-17	14	0
2017-18	11	11
2018-19	8	8
2019-20	12	9
2020-21	0	0
Total	45	28

Source: See www.gov.uk/government/publications/tackling-alcohol-smuggling-outputs

Counterfeit alcohol

As discussed above, counterfeiting is used to describe the marketing of alcohol in ways that infringe trademarks. The counterfeit product may contain either legally produced, or illegally produced, alcohol. Some illicit traders produce alcohol illegally without infringing trademarks to meet demand for low-cost products which are sold unbranded, or under brand names that are unregistered. The price gap between the latter products and licit products can be sizeable due to the taxes that are imposed on the licit products, enticing some consumers to knowingly opt for the much cheaper, illegal product, even though it may pose health risks.

The OECD has carried out much work on counterfeiting, including a 2008 study which looked specifically at the situation in food and drink (OECD, 2008[8]). The study provides a framework for assessing the attractiveness of a product for counterfeiters. It argues that the decision of a party to engage in the production of counterfeit or pirated goods involves i) an assessment of the nature and profitability of the market for fakes, ii) the complexity and cost of the production and distribution of the fake products, and iii) the risk and consequences of detection. Counterfeiting provides parties engaging in the practice with increased opportunities to profit from illicit trade, even though they are subject to additional penalties if their operations are disrupted by law enforcement.

Characteristics of markets for counterfeits

With respect to the nature of the market, it is presumed that counterfeiters would focus their efforts on the primary market, in which consumers buy a counterfeit believing it is genuine. The secondary market, where consumers would knowingly purchase a fake product, is presumed to be small. There are exceptions, however, such as markets where poverty is a driver for illicit consumption and people knowingly buy counterfeit alcohol.

The counterfeiters would therefore focus their efforts almost exclusively on deceiving consumers. From a value perspective, this makes sense, because counterfeiters can charge higher prices for goods that consumers believe to be genuine, rather than ones that consumers know are fake. The economics of counterfeiting are viewed as very attractive as i) the market is large and growing, ii) brands are strong and iii) profitability can be quite high as prestigious products are sold at high premiums over lesser products. Even within brands, price disparities can be quite high. A bottle of a highly sought wine, for example, might cost thousands of dollars for a banner year, while other vintages might sell for several hundred.

Production, technology and distribution of counterfeits

The counterfeiting of alcohol can take various forms.[4] In the case of wine and spirits, parties sometimes produce look-alike products that are intended to deceive buyers while not necessarily infringing trademarks. These products can enter the markets through an array of channels, ranging from local stores, to bars, cafes and street markets, and supply channels are globalized, relying on numerous logistical solutions. Box 3.2 provides some specific examples of enforcement action dealing with counterfeit alcohol.

Another form of counterfeiting involves bottle tampering, where parties collect and refill genuine proprietary bottles with cheaper wine and spirits.[5] While this procedure is longstanding, counterfeiters have increased their attention to it, finding it worthwhile to obtain and refill genuine empty bottles of high-end wines and spirits, rather than to try to replicate original glass bottles. In addition, counterfeiters have started to turn towards manufacturing their own "fake" glass bottles as there is a shortage of empty genuine bottles. In these cases, original genuine labels are usually still attached to the bottles. This approach has also greatly accelerated their "time to market", making it possible to make a dramatic impact in a very short time potentially in any market in the world. The economics of such tampering are attractive. Refilling a bottle of an expensive vintage Château Lafite Rothschild, even with a comparable product, can be highly profitable. Moreover, it could well be that only a handful of consumers would be able to detect the fraud. Interest in refilling genuine bottles with less expensive beverages has resulted in strong demand for empty bottles of famous wines and premium spirits. In response, some European wine and spirits exporters have been campaigning for restaurants to destroy bottles after the genuine beverage has been consumed so that they cannot be refilled, and to ensure that caps are destroyed as well so that they cannot be illicitly reused.

Counterfeiting can also be carried out using illegally produced alcohol. Such production can be carried out on a small scale, with minimal investment, but there are examples of more sophisticated and grander scale operations that are capable of producing 10 000 bottles of alcohol per hour (Skehan, Sanchez and Hastings, 2016[9]). There can thus be significant disparities in the cost and technologies employed to produce the alcohol. Similarly, it could be quite easy to conceal small scale "basement" operations, while there could be challenges with higher volume, large operations. With respect to small scale production, equipment for producing whiskey, scotch, rum, tequila, vodka and the like that then can be sold as counterfeit, can be easily purchased on Internet platforms, starting at prices slightly more than USD 100. The producers of counterfeit alcohol can free-ride weakly controlled distribution channels to buy raw ingredients such as ethanol. On the supply side, the illicit traders can expand their activities by selling directly to consumers through informal outlets, duty-free areas, and e-commerce platforms.

Legal frameworks to prevent counterfeiting

The ability of law enforcement to detect and intercept counterfeit and illegally produced alcohol is limited, particularly to the extent that products are shipped locally (thereby avoiding customs scrutiny), in small quantities, and are distributed to parties which are complicit in the fraud.

In the case of illegal production, if operations are discovered, the parties involved may be subject to criminal penalties and fines. In the United States, for example, parties involved in the illegal production of spirits are subject, under federal law, to imprisonment of up to 5 years, and/or fines of up to USD 10 000;[6] in Australia the penalties are fines of up to AUD 85 000 or more or 2 years imprisonment,[7] while in Canada fines of CAD 500 to 10 000 are imposed and/or imprisonment of up to 12 months.[8]

Box 3.2. Examples of counterfeit alcohol in global markets

- **China** (cognac). The ringleader of a Chinese counterfeiting gang was sentenced to 15 years in prison for producing fake Hennessy Cognac by substituting with Louis Royer.[1] The gang comprised a group of counterfeits producers and distributors who began running the scam in 2017. They set up a factory and hired a "blending master" to help create the fake Hennessy Cognac by using Louis Royer Cognac as the base ingredient, topping it with caramel coloring. The total sales amount of the scam reached RMB 3.4 million.

- **Ireland** (wine). Irish customs seized 24,750 litres of counterfeit wine worth EUR 302 000 in March 2021. The wine represented a loss to the Exchequer of around EUR 161 500.[2] In 2020, Irish revenue officials reportedly carried out some 1,808 seizures of alcohol finding 764,174 litres of counterfeit alcohol worth EUR 4.17 million.

- **Italy** (wine). Italian authorities broke up a ring the had been bottling and labelling fake bottles of Super Tuscan wine from different vintages between 2010 and 2015.[3] The police were able to intercept a delivery of 41 cases of what claimed to be Sassicaia 2015. It was estimated that the counterfeiters were selling around 700 cases of the fake wine per month, a total of 4 200 bottles worth around EUR 400 000. According to their investigations, several customers from countries including Korea, China and Russia, had already placed orders for a thousand cases, priced at 70% below the market value. The wine used in the counterfeit products is thought to have originated from Sicily, the bottles from Turkey and the fake labels, caps, crates and tissue paper from Bulgaria.

- **Spain** (rum). Spanish authorities seized over 225 000 bottles of counterfeit rum worth EUR 3.5 million and arrested 24 people believed to be part of an international counterfeiting ring.[4] The rum was sold under three different brands. Investigation revealed that the spirits were made in the Dominican Republic, bottled in Honduras in bottles that came from China and completed with counterfeit labels produced in Peru. The goods were then sent to Spain via tax warehouses in the Netherlands. The investigation resulted in Honduran authorities intercepting two containers loaded with fake rum with an estimated value of EUR 500 000. In total, law enforcement officers investigated 50 Spanish, Portuguese and Dutch companies as part of the operation.

- **Scotland** (vodka). Bottles of vodka laced with a potentially lethal antifreeze ingredient were seized from a shop and pub in Scotland. the seized bottles of counterfeit vodka were believed to contain isopropanol, which is used in anti-freeze.[5]

- **United Kingdom** (wine). Bottles of fake YellowTail Merlot, Cabernet Sauvignon, Shiraz and Pinot Grigio were found in shops across the country. The wines are said to have convincing labels that were deceiving UK retailers. The operation was suspected of being large-scale,

---

> probably originating abroad, using organized crime gangs in the country to distribute and sell the products.[6]
>
> - **Ireland (beer).** More than 25 400 liters of illicit beer has been seized by customs officials at Dublin Port. The Perla branded drinks were worth about €101 300 and represented a potential tax loss of €47 400. The cargo was found during a search of a Romanian registered truck and trailer that had disembarked a ferry from Wales.
>
> Notes: 1 See www.thedrinksbusiness.com/2021/03/hennessy-cognac-fraudster-sentenced-in-china/.
> 2 See www.thedrinksbusiness.com/2021/03/irish-customs-seize-counterfeit-wine-worth-e302000-in-cork/.
> 3 See www.thedrinksbusiness.com/2020/10/italian-police-bust-e2m-fake-sassicaia-ring/)
> 4 See www.thedrinksbusiness.com/2021/01/spanish-authorities-seize-e3-5m-worth-of-fake-rum/.
> 5 See (www.thedrinksbusiness.com/2019/12/antifreeze-laced-vodka-seized-in-fife/.
> 6 See www.thedrinksbusiness.com/2021/02/uk-being-flooded-with-fake-yellowtail-wines/.

With respect to counterfeits, the shipment of dry goods for counterfeits (labels, bottles) can go undetected by customs in most cases. The level of enforcement is also an issue as it varies among jurisdictions, as do the penalties that are applied. If intercepted, counterfeit goods can be confiscated and destroyed, while rights holders can be compensated for damages. As mentioned above, custodial sentences for counterfeit crimes are rare and the ultimate beneficiaries are rarely prosecuted. Moreover, in many countries the prosecution of counterfeiters is a complicated endeavour.

While enforcement may not be effective or sufficiently deterrent in some countries, the penalties on the books for counterfeiting, however, are not insignificant. This is because counterfeiting is deemed a criminal activity in most countries, exposing parties engaged in the activity to the possibility of significant prison terms and fines. In most countries, the length of prison terms is discretionary, bounded by ceilings (Table 3.9). In the case of the United States, for example, criminal groups who are repeat offenders can be imprisoned for up to 20 years, which is the most severe potential sanction among countries. On the other hand, maximum sentences in Australia, Brazil, Canada, Germany and India range from 1 to 5 years. In addition to prison terms, fines can be imposed on the counterfeiters. As with prison terms, the fines are generally subject to ceilings, which range from several thousand dollars in some countries, to USD 15 million in the United States. Importantly, fines can be imposed in lieu of prison terms in most countries. Lesser penalties are imposed by many countries on counterfeiting which involves individuals or minor infractions.

Table 3.9 Criminal sanctions and fines for trademark infringement in selected countries

Years of possible imprisonment and fines

Country	Years	Note
Australia	< 5	Up to 5 years or AUD 122 100 (550 penalty units), or both; minor infractions up to 12 months or AUD 13 320 (60 penalty units), or both.
Brazil	< 1	Depending on the circumstances, from 3 months to 1 year, or from 1 to 3 months; in both cases a fine can be imposed instead.
Canada	< 5	Not more than 5 years or a fine of not more than CAD 1 000 000, or both; for minor infractions, not more than six months or a fine of not than CAD 25 000, or both.
China	< 10	3 years or less for serious infringement, or a fine, or both; 3 to 10 years for very serious infringement, with a fine. The fine can amount to up to 5 times the illicit gain realised.
France	< 7	Depending on the circumstances, up to: 3 years and EUR 300 000 or 4 years and EUR 400 000 for natural persons; 7 years and EUR 750 000 if committed by a criminal organisation or online to the public. The fine amounts are multiplied by five when the offender is a legal entity.
Germany	< 5	Between 3 months and 5 years, if infringement is on commercial basis, or a gang is involved; up to 3 years or a monetary fine for simple offences.
India	< 3	Unless the court finds special circumstances, not less than 6 months or more than 3 years, plus a fine of not less than INR 50 000 or more than INR 200 000.
Japan	< 10	For direct infringement, not more than 10 years or a fine not exceeding JPY 10 000 000 yen, or a

Country	Years	Note
		combination thereof. For indirect infringement not more than 5 years or a fine not exceeding JPY 5 000 000 yen, or a combination thereof.
United Kingdom	< 10	Not more than 10 years, or a fine, or both; for minor infractions, not more than 6 months, or a fine, or both.
United States	< 20	For parties other than individuals, not more than 20 years or a fine of not more than USD 15 million, or both, for i) repeat offenders and ii) cases involving serious bodily injury or death, except in the case of death, life imprisonment is possible. Otherwise, for parties other than individuals, not more than 10 years or a fine of not more than USD 5 million. For individuals, not more than 10 years or a fine of not more than USD 2 000 000, or both, for fist offences; for repeat offences and offences involving serious bodily injury or death, not more than 20 years or a fine of not more than USD 5 million, or both, except that in the case of death, life imprisonment is possible. .

Source: (Merchant&Gould, 2021[10]), https://asic.gov.au/about-asic/asic-investigations-and-enforcement/fines-and-penalties/, and www.chinaiplawupdate.com/2020/12/chinas-national-peoples-congress-passes-amended-criminal-law-adding-an-economic-espionage-article-and-increasing-prison-time-for-intellectual-property-crimes/.

Impact of COVID-19 on illicit trade in alcohol

The pandemic has had a significant effect on alcohol consumption patterns as restaurants and bars have often closed and lockdowns affected the ability of consumers to shop for products in their usual manner, while supply chains have also been affected by border closures and government measures that have both liberalized some aspects of the market (especially with respect to home delivery), while tightening others (to, for example, discourage excessive consumption). Essentially, the measures that were taken by countries in response to the pandemic tended to limit the availability of alcohol, providing an important opening for illicit traders and criminal organizations alike to step up the scale of their operations and increase prices, thereby undermining the efforts of governments to effectively manage the crisis.

Consumption

While markets and supply chains were disrupted during the pandemic, consumer drinking habits were largely unchanged. This was confirmed in surveys carried out during the first wave (13-21 May 2020) in nine countries,[9] which indicated that most drinkers did not change their underlying drinking habits (Table 3.10). This was true for all of the countries surveyed, except Mexico and South Africa, where changes in habits were more pronounced. A survey of 14 countries[10] carried out during the second wave (30 October-11 November 2020), mirrored the results of the first in most respects.

Table 3.10. Survey of drinking habits during the pandemic during the first and second waves (percent of respondents)

Drinking habits during pandemic	First wave		Second wave	
	Average, 9 countries	Country range	Average, 14 countries	Country range
Drinking more	8	3-15	8	4-13
Drinking same	39	14-46	42	29-56
Drinking less	15	9-24	18	12-30
Stopped drinking	6	1-32	4	2-9
Started drinking	1	0-2	1	0-3
Non-drinker	29	21-40	25	15-38
Other	2	-	2	-
Total	100	-	100	-

Notes: First wave survey: 13-21 May 2020 ; Second wave survey: 30 October-11 November 2020.
Source: see IARD, www.iard.org/science-resources/detail/Consumption-of-Alcohol-during-COVID-19-pandemic.

Restrictions

Markets were disrupted as a result of restrictions introduced on alcohol sales in many countries (OECD, 2021[11]). Some countries enacted measures to limit production and/or consumption of alcohol. In most cases, however, restrictions limited the sale of alcohol and put constraints on venues where alcohol could be consumed. In a few instances, governments implemented nationwide or regional alcohol bans during lockdown periods. India, Panama and South Africa, for example, implemented extended total nationwide bans, while a number of countries, such as Sri Lanka, Zimbabwe and French Polynesia introduced bans that were quickly reversed (Box 3.3) (TRACIT, 2021[12]). In Mexico all breweries were closed for over a month, except for exports. Dry laws that put restrictions on hours of sale or prohibitions on the sale and consumption of alcohol were implemented in some local jurisdictions.

Box 3.3. Covid-related alcohol bans in India, Panama and South Africa in 2020

India

The National Disaster Management Authority of India (NDMA) issued an order on 24 March 2020 directing the National Government, States and Union Territories to take "effective measures so as to prevent the spread of COVID19 in the country." Later the same day, elucidating the NDMA Order, the Ministry of Home Affairs (MHA) issued mandatory Guidelines for States containing a list of permitted essential goods and services that effectively banned the sale of alcohol as a non-essential commodity. The ban was in place until May 4 when the MHA issued new guidelines permitting certain types of liquor shops to open and allowing individual States to decide for themselves whether to resume alcohol sales. In addition, in some states excise taxes on alcohol were increased.

Panama

On 24 March 2020, Panama issued Executive Decree 507 which enacted a nation-wide ban on the distribution, sale and consumption of alcoholic beverages throughout the national territory. The dry law was partially relaxed on 8 May, through Executive Decree 612, which limited the sale of alcoholic beverages to either one bottle of wine or spirit or one six of pack of beer per person. The restrictions lasted until 18 June, when the State of National Emergency was lifted.

South Africa

South Africa's nation-wide ban on all domestic and export sales of alcohol products and production and transportation of alcohol products went into effect when the country went into a coronavirus lockdown on 26 March 2020 and lasted until 17 August, with a six-week relaxation from 1 June to 12 July. Effective on 8 August, the sale of alcohol was permitted again in "licensed premises for off-consumption, from 09h00 to 17h00, from Mondays to Thursdays, excluding Fridays, Saturdays, Sundays and public holidays".

Source: (TRACIT, 2021[12])

The restrictions had significant consequences for economies, including i) increased traffic in illicit alcohol, ii) increased exposure to health risks from the consumption of substandard illicit products, including hospitalization and deaths, iii) decreased tax revenues from the sale of alcohol and iv) damage to the alcohol industry due to lower sales.

Impact on illicit trade

With respect to traffic in illicit alcohol, the restrictions were followed by an uptick in the production and distribution of illicit alcohol in many countries (TRACIT, 2021[12]).

As discussed above, with the closure of many bars and restaurants, counterfeiters of spirits were not able to source genuine empty bottles in the markets, so the new "modus operandi" became the manufacture of fake glass bottles. This greatly accelerated the ability of counterfeiters to make a dramatic impact in a very short time potentially in any market in the world. So, we've witnessed the emergence of the production of counterfeit at scale in markets, where it wasn't an issue previously.

In the area of smuggling the situation worsened as well. Multiple sales bans, restrictions on the availability of alcohol and tax increases on legitimate operators resulted in consumers looking for alternatives on the black market, with unfortunate consequences for the health of the consumers, legitimate alcohol producers and government tax revenue collection. The hospitality sector globally suffered to the point where their survival was threatened; this state of economic despair served as a catalyst for some of them to acquire illicit alcohol to try to facilitate their financial recovery.

In India, seizures of illicit alcohol increased significantly; many people were arrested for producing illicit products, while some genuine, licit products were resold by scalpers at high prices. In South Africa, counterfeit vodka operations were uncovered, and the smuggling of products from neighboring countries increased. Moreover, there were instances in which counterfeiters targeted manufacturers, stealing bottle caps which would later be used in the refilling of used, branded bottles with illegal alcohol; the bottles would be resealed and sold to consumers as original product (OECD, 2021[11]). In Mexico, as a result of the restrictions on formal distribution channels, illegal vendors stepped in to supply the unmet demand through illegal stores and unregulated marketplaces, introducing toxic contraband and counterfeit products onto the market. Just in May 2020, 70 persons died due to illicit alcohol consumption in the state of Puebla.[11]

In Panama, officials at the country's free trade zone reported that counterfeit and artisanal production of alcoholic beverages had skyrocketed in response to reduced availability in traditional supply chains (TRACIT, 2021[12]). In Sri Lanka, the Department of Excise reported that the ban on alcohol led to a 500% escalation in the production of illicit alcohol; moreover, police reported over 18 000 instances of illicit alcoholic drinks being produced following the introduction of a Covid-related ban.

Impact on health

Alcohol poisoning and death related to the introduction of alcohol restrictions were reported in a number of countries, including Botswana, Colombia, Costa Rica, Honduras, India, Mexico and South Africa (TRACIT, 2021[12]). More than 300 people have lost their lives due to illicit alcohol consumption in the Dominican Republic in 2020. There is also recent news that more than 100 people have died from drinking illegal alcohol in India and more than 200 in Mexico. These all-too-common incidents show both the serious consequences of illegal alcohol production. These people die because of the actions of unscrupulous bootleggers, who produce and sell poisonous alcoholic beverages that contain methanol – which can kill even in very small quantities – can cause blindness, or organ damage. The public health costs and personal tragedies from illicit alcohol are staggering. Other health impacts included the effects of alcohol withdrawal on some persons who were unable to purchase products (reported in India and Mexico), and the risky behavior of persons who engaged in panic buying in crowded environments (reported in Thailand). Moreover, persons in the Dominican Republic, Iran, Peru and Turkey reportedly died after drinking dangerous alcoholic products in the mistaken belief that they would be effective in countering the Covid virus.

Impact on government revenue

Excise and related taxes are an important source of revenue in many countries, so the reduction in collections due to restrictions had a significant impact on budgets. Millions in losses were reported in Colombia, India, Kenya, Mexico, Panama, South Africa, Sri Lanka and the United States (in the state of Pennsylvania) (TRACIT, 2021[12]). In South Africa, the first and second alcohol bans resulted in an estimated loss of direct tax (excluding excise) of ZAR 7.8 billion and a further direct excise loss of ZAR 5.8 billion (OECD, 2021[11]).

Impact on business

Restrictions had far-reaching effects on employment, sales, profits and investment at companies in the industry. Specific examples were reported in a number of countries, including Australia, Colombia, India, Kenya, Mexico, South Africa and Trinidad and Tobago (TRACIT, 2021[12]). In South Africa, an estimated 165 000 jobs were lost in the sector as a result of the first and second alcohol bans, and two major producers announced cancellation of planned investment in new plants (OECD, 2021[11]) and (TRACIT, 2021[12]).

References

ACEA (2021), *Vehicles in Use*, European Automobile Manufacturers Association, Brussels, https://www.acea.auto/files/report-vehicles-in-use-europe-january-2021-1.pdf. [6]

Ellis, C. (2017), *On Tap Europe: Organised Crime and Illicit Trade in Tobacco, Alcohol and Pharmaceuticals*, RUSI (Royal United Services Institute), https://static.rusi.org/201703_rusi_whr_2-17_on_tap_europe_updated_low-res.pdf. [7]

Euromonitor International (2018), *Size and Shape of the Global Illicit Alcohol Market*, Euromonitor International, https://go.euromonitor.com/white-paper-alcoholic-drinks-2018-size-and-shape-of-the-global-illicit-alcohol-market.html?refresh=1. [2]

Merchant&Gould (2021), *Criminal Liability for Trademark Infringement: A Collaborative International Study*, http://www.vda.pt/xms/files/05_Publicacoes/2021/CriminalLiabilityForTrademarkInfringement.pdf. [10]

Ngo Anh P. et al. (2021), *"Alcohol excise taxes as a percentage of retail alcohol prices in 26 OECD countries"*, Drug and Alcohol Dependence, https://doi.org/10.1016/j.drugalcdep.2020.108415. [5]

OECD (2021), *Crisis policy, illicit alcohol and lessons learned from lockdown*, OECD, http://www.oecd.org/gov/illicit-trade/summary-note-crisis-policy-illicit-alcohol.pdf. [11]

OECD (2020), *Consumption Tax Trends 2020: VAT/GST and Excise Rates, Trends and Policy Issues*, OECD Publishing, Paris, https://doi.org/10.1787/152def2d-en. [4]

OECD (2008), *The Economic Impact of Counterfeiting and Piracy*, OECD Publishing, Paris, https://doi.org/10.1787/9789264045521-en. [8]

Skehan, P., I. Sanchez and L. Hastings (2016), "The size, impacts and drivers of illicit trade in alcohol", in *Illicit Trade: Converging Criminal Networks*, OECD Publishing, Paris, https://doi.org/10.1787/9789264251847-10-en. [9]

TRACIT (2021), *Prohibition, Illicit Alcohol and Lessons Learned from Lockdown*, Transnational Alliance to Combat Illicit Trade, https://www.tracit.org/uploads/1/0/2/2/102238034/tracit_prohibition_illicit_alcohol_and_lessons_learned_from_lockdown_jan2021_hr.pdf. [12]

WCO (2020), *Illicit Trade Report 2019*, World Customs Organization, Brussels, http://www.wcoomd.org/-/media/wco/public/global/pdf/topics/enforcement-and-compliance/activities-and-programmes/illicit-trade-report/itr_2019_en.pdf?db=web. [3]

WHO (2018), *Global status report on alcohol and health*, World Health Organization, Geneva, https://apps.who.int/iris/rest/bitstreams/1151838/retrieve. [1]

Notes

[1] Little should be read into the decline, given the high variability of seizure data from years to year, and he changes in the number of countries reporting such data from year to year.

[2] See OECD (2018), Governance Frameworks to Counter Illicit Trade, Illicit Trade, OECD Publishing, Paris, https://doi.org/10.1787/9789264291652-en

[3] See OECD 2021, Crisis policy, illicit alcohol and Lessons learned from lockdown. Charis notw. Available here: https://www.oecd.org/gov/illicit-trade/summary-note-crisis-policy-illicit-alcohol.pdf

[4] See www.researchandmarkets.com/reports/3507849/wines-and-spirits-anti-counterfeit-and-brandhttps://www.researchandmarkets.com/reports/3507849/wines-and-spirits-anti-counterfeit-and-brand.

[5] See www.researchandmarkets.com/reports/3507849/wines-and-spirits-anti-counterfeit-and-brandhttps://www.researchandmarkets.com/reports/3507849/wines-and-spirits-anti-counterfeit-and-brand

[6] See www.ttb.gov/distilled-spirits/penalties-for-illegal-distilling

[7] See https://ramsdenlaw.com.au/news/distilling-alcohol-spirits-liquor-in-australia.

[8] See https://laws-lois.justice.gc.ca/eng/acts/E-14/page-11.html#h-184253.

[9] Australia, France, Germany, Japan, Mexico, New Zealand, South Africa, United Kingdom and the United States.

[10] Australia, Czech Republic, France Germany, Italy, Japan, Mexico, Netherland, New Zealand, South Africa, Spain Sweden, United Kingdom and the United States.

[11] See: https://www.lajornadadeoriente.com.mx/puebla/ingesta-de-alcohol-adulterado-en-el-seco/.

4 Direct impacts of illicit trade in alcohol

This chapter deals with the impacts of illicit trade in alcohol and shows that it can affect economies in a number of ways, including through effects on consumer health and government revenues, as well as impacts on legitimate producers and on efforts to pursue sustainable development goals, which are compromised due to the role of organised crime in the market.

Consumer health

Illicit and other forms of unrecorded alcohol are commonly the cheapest form of alcohol and have been associated with heavy drinking patterns. The illicit products are often consumed by more vulnerable populations, such as people of low socioeconomic status, rural populations, and people with alcohol dependence (Probst Charlotte et al., 2019[1]). They are thus more vulnerable in two ways: i) their consumption may be higher than would otherwise be the case with fully taxed beverages an ii) they would be more susceptible to purchasing tainted products from unscrupulous parties. In general, the biggest health concern with respect to illicit alcohol is consumer exposure to health risks associated with toxic illicit alternatives. Beyond the fact that these illicit substitutes do not comply with sanitary, quality and safety regulations, the most hazardous are contaminated with toxic chemical additives. According to WHO, "consumption of illicitly or informally produced alcohol could have [...] negative health consequences due to higher ethanol content and potential contamination with toxic substances, such as methanol.[1] The use of methanol in the production of illicit alcohol is particularly alarming, as it has a strong causal connection to morbidity and mortality; it can result in a decreased level of consciousness, poor or no co-ordination, vomiting, abdominal pain, permanent blindness and death (Lachenmeier Dirk W. Maria Neufeld and Jürgen Rehm, 2021[2]). Moreover, inferior distillation processes used by counterfeiters can introduce methanol or fail to sufficiently remove methanol from final products. This can result from the methanol or toxic denaturants present in these products as a result of the production or manufacturing processes utilised. That is, the fermented mash may be a substance which has high levels of methanol due to the distillation process, or the illicit alcohol may reflect a failed attempt to remove methanol from denatured or wood alcohol, or the fake alcohol may result from the blending of industrial alcohol (that is, alcohol containing methanol or other toxic denaturant materials) with other substances.[2]

It has been estimated that ethanol as a component of unrecorded alcohol could be responsible for approximately 750 000 to 800 000 deaths per year, compared to several thousand per year in the case of methanol. Instances of the adverse effects of tainted alcohol on consumers are regularly reported in the press, and health ministries in many countries have issued warnings about the consequences of drinking such alcohol (see Box 4.1).

Another potential source of harm comes from the addition of accelerants during fermentation. There are reports of animal carcasses, fecal matter, even barbed wire and other inappropriate additives that can increase health risk. In some parts of the world clandestine production equipment may include oil drums and containers previously used for chemicals, all increasing risk of contamination and toxicity to the consumer.

Box 4.1. Examples of methanol poisoning

An outbreak of methanol poisoning occurred from 17-26 December 2016, in the Siberian city of Irkutsk, when 123 people drank a spirits and surrogate mixture that contained methanol. Of the 123 who were poisoned, 76 died. Before this, a series of methanol poisonings occurred in Eastern Ukraine killing at least 38 people.

A methanol-poisoning outbreak occurred in the Czech Republic in 2012 from counterfeit alcohol and resulted in 140 people suffering health damage and more than 50 deaths. The mass poisoning in the Czech Republic was associated with a significant decrease of health-related quality of life for the survivors), as well as to long-term costs for the healthcare system.

Methanol in levels associated with health risk (average concentration: 23%) was identified in 4 of 877 samples in Iran. Although the sources of the methanol in the noncommercial beverages were not provided, a mixture of chemically pure methanol is assumed, as natural levels of methanol at such high concentrations in alcoholic fermentations appear to be impossible.

In a large sampling of illegal beverages by the police in India, 3 of 1,221 samples (0.25%) were found to contain methanol (no ethanol) with concentrations in toxic ranges (70%–92%).

In April 2021, during the height of the COVID-19 pandemic, methanol poisoning resulted in the death of 26 persons, while more than 80 persons suffered adverse effects from drinking illegally produced alcohol in the Dominican Republic. Two possible sources were identified; a homemade adulterated drink known as clerén and the other is a type of frozen cocktail. Clerén is an illegal alcoholic beverage without a health registration that is sold in bulk and consumed by poor people, because of its low cost. Officials also suspected that some bottles of recognized alcohol brands in the Dominican Republic were refilled with product containing methanol.

Also, during the pandemic, in Russia, 34 persons died from drinking illicit vodka containing methanol in October 2021, with another 25 hospitalized. Police investigation discovered a warehouse manufacturing plant in which over 600 litres of alcoholic spirits were seized, with a further 1,279 bottles of counterfeit alcohol discovered in the region affected by the contaminated alcohol during two days of widespread checks.

Source: (Lachenmeier Dirk W. Maria Neufeld and Jürgen Rehm, 2021[2]), Zamani et al., 2019, www.foodsafetynews.com/2021/04/deaths-in-dominican-republic-linked-to-tainted-alcohol/ and www.brusselstimes.com/news/188971/counterfeit-alcohol-in-russia-claims-34-lives/.

Other potentially toxic ingredients found in illicit alcohol include formic acid, which is contained in some antiseptic medicinal surrogates (Lachenmeier Dirk W. Maria Neufeld and Jürgen Rehm, 2021[2]). Formic acid can lead to exacerbation of the chronic effects of ethanol by contributing to an excessive buildup of acid in the body (metabolic acidosis). Some of the toxicological studies from Kazakhstan, Russia, and Ukraine indicate that patients treated for acute poisonings with alcohol not meant for human consumption also showed traces of methanol, isopropanol, acetone, fusel alcohols, bio-solvents, and unknown and unidentified alcohols.

Other contaminants found in unrecorded alcohol include aflatoxins (i.e. toxins produced by certain fungi that are found on agricultural crops such as maize, peanuts, cottonseed, and tree nuts), hydrocyanic acid (a highly poisonous hydrogen cyanide product), cyanide derivatives (including ethyl carbamate), heavy metal contamination (with lead, arsenic, or cadmium), and elevated levels of acetaldehyde (which might contribute to the carcinogenicity of ethanol) (Lachenmeier Dirk W. Maria Neufeld and Jürgen Rehm, 2021[2]).

It should be noted that consumers are often deceived and uncertain about the legality of a product. Consumers do not always know when they are purchasing an illicit alcoholic beverage or how to identify one. To make matters more difficult, vendors sometimes sell a mix of licit and illicit products. In addition, as discussed earlier, illicit players use various methods to make products appear legitimate, such as refilling bottles of legitimately branded beverages with cheaper illicit alcohol, or counterfeiting packaging labels and fiscal stamps. To address this problem, some licit alcohol manufacturers and other organizations have invested in communications campaigns to help consumers learn about the characteristics that may indicate a beverage is illicit (e.g. unusually low prices, damaged labels or seals, dirty bottles, cloudy liquid, etc.).

Impact on legitimate producers

Counterfeit, smuggling and other forms of illicit alcohol can lower the sales and profit of branded products, with severe consequences for legitimate business and for their workers on a commercial basis.

First, legal operators are not able to compete on a level-playing field with illicit trades who evade taxes, particularly those operators whose products are taxed at disproportionate rates. Illicit producers and traders are not subject to the costs associated with running of legitimate businesses (including wages, health securities, operational and marketing costs). In addition, the cost of raw materials is lower for illicit producers, particularly if they are using denatured alcohol as a starting point for production, free from taxes, and also without the need for a lengthy fermentation and distillation process. It means that they can either offer customers a lower price or commercialize the products at a similar price, while having much higher margins. The existing OECD evidence highlights the negative impacts that counterfeiting has on legitimate producers. It also points to strong growth in the trade and production of counterfeit alcohol, especially during the pandemic.[3]

Second, the level of illicit trade in a given country is an important consideration for legitimate operators when taking a decision on whether to enter a market, and whether to invest in production and distribution in that market.

There is also the reputational cost to legitimate producers from consumer dissatisfaction with counterfeit products or the perception that a brand is likely to be counterfeit, eroding trust and reducing sales. Campaigns to combat illicit products can also affect producers, by shifting resources to the campaigns and, in the process, by adding to corporate costs.

Government revenue

The most direct way that government misses out on revenue is the extent to which illicit alcohol does not pay taxes. Within this, there are the taxes particular to alcohol (excise taxes) that represent a large part of the difference in price between illicit alcohol and legal alcohol. This is the situation for all forms of illicit alcohol, noting that the health risks represent additional risk on top for the forms of illicit alcohol that are not just tax leakage or smuggled. On top of excise, there are other general sales taxes that would likely not be paid, depending on the route by which illicit alcohol is sold. Mitigating illicit trade therefore presents a certain challenge to address the potentially growth in demand for illicit untaxed products. Likewise, employment taxes and corporate taxes are not likely to be paid by criminal organisations involved in illicit alcohol.

In addition to lost VAT, tariff and excise taxes, taxes paid by legitimate producers may be diminished to the extent that sales and profits of legitimate products decline. In the case of the United Kingdom, HM Revenue & Customs noted that alcohol excise taxes amounted to GBP 10.5 billion in 2015, which represented 2% of total UK tax receipts. At the same time, illicit alcohol was estimated to have cost the treasury some GBP 1.2 billion (HM Revenue & Customs, 2016[3]). A 2018 study by IARD of the situation in a number of countries estimated lost tax revenues of more than USD 1.8 billion in the countries studied (IARD, 2018[4]) (Table 4.1). A separate study by Euromonitor calculated the fiscal loss in 20 Latin American, Eastern European and African countries to be on the order of USD 3.6 billion (Euromonitor International, 2018[5]).[4]

Table 4.1. Fiscal loss from illicit alcohol in selected countries

Millions of USD

Region/Country	Fiscal loss	Year
Africa:		
Cameroon	112	2014
Mozambique	344	2018
South Africa	800	2020
Tanzania	110	2015
Uganda	172	2015
Zambia	51	2014
Europe:		
Czech Republic	99	2014
Latin America:		
Colombia	406	2015
Costa Rica	75	2014
Dominican Republic	262	2016
Ecuador	118	2015
El Salvador	16	2015
Honduras	6	2015
Mexico	7	2013
Panama	6	2015
Peru	80.6	2015
Suriname	9	2016
Trinidad and Tobago	9	2013
Asia		
Indonesia	69	2018
Vietnam	441	2019
Total of above	3,192.60	

Source: (IARD, 2018[6]) and Euromonitor.

References

Euromonitor International (2018), *Illicit Alcohol Research Review*, Euromonitor International, http://www.tracit.org/uploads/1/0/2/2/102238034/illicit_alcohol_meta_study_-_euromonitor_.pdf. [5]

Euromonitor, I. (2018), *Análisis del Mercado Ilegal de Bebidas Alcohólicas en México*, Euromonitor International, http://www.tracit.org/uploads/1/0/2/2/102238034/cerveceros-alcohol_ilegal_mexico_final_2018.pdf. [16]

Euromonitor, I. (2017), *Análisis del Mercado Ilegal de Bebidas Alcohólicas en Bolivia*, Euromonitor International, http://www.tracit.org/uploads/1/0/2/2/102238034/an%C3%A1lisis_del_mercado_iegal_de_bebidas_alcoholicas_en_bolivia_2017.pdf. [18]

Euromonitor, I. (2017), *Illegal Alcohol in Dominican Republic*, Euromonitor International, http://www.tracit.org/uploads/1/0/2/2/102238034/emi_cnd_illegal_alcohol_market_in_dr_final_report_2017.pdf. [13]

Euromonitor, I. (2016), *Análisis del Mercado Ilegal de Bebidas Alcohólicas en Guatemala*, Euromonitor International, http://www.tracit.org/uploads/1/0/2/2/102238034/emi_illegal_alcohol_in_gt_presentation_final_2016.pdf. [17]

Euromonitor, I. (2016), *Market Analysis for Illicit Alcohol in Malawi*, Euromonitor International, http://www.tracit.org/uploads/1/0/2/2/102238034/illicit_alcohol_malawi_-_final_2016.pdf. [11]

Euromonitor, I. (2016), *Mercado de Bebidas Alcoholicas Ilegales en Colombia, Ecuador y Peru*, Euromonitor International, http://www.tracit.org/uploads/1/0/2/2/102238034/illegal_alcohol_in_copec_final_report_2018.pdf. [9]

Euromonitor, I. (2016), *The Illegal Alcoholic Beverages Market in Six Latin American Countries 2015: Colombia, Ecuador, El Salvador, Honduras, Panama and Peru*, Euromonitor International, http://www.tracit.org/uploads/1/0/2/2/102238034/illegal_alcohol_in_latam_full_report_2016_en.pdf. [8]

Euromonitor, I. (2015), *Analysis of Illicit Alcohol in the Czech Republic*, Euromonitor International, http://www.tracit.org/uploads/1/0/2/2/102238034/euromonitor_illicit_alcohol_in_cz_-_report_2015.pdf. [14]

Euromonitor, I. (2015), *Illicit Alcohol in Russia*, Euromonitor International, http://www.tracit.org/uploads/1/0/2/2/102238034/illicit_alcohol_market_in_russia_report_2015_full_report.pdf. [12]

Euromonitor, I. (2014), *Análisis del Mercado Ilegal de Bebidas Alcohólicas en Argentina*, Euromonitor International, https://www.tracit.org/uploads/1/0/2/2/102238034/alcohol_ilegal_argentina-_9.11.14.pdf. [19]

HM Revenue & Customs (2016), *The HMRC Alcohol Strategy: Modernising alcohol taxes to tackle fraud and reduce burdens on alcohol businesses*, HM Revenue & Customs, https://assets.publishing.service.gov.uk/government/uploads/system/uploads/attachment_data/file/510235/HMRC_Alcohol_Strategy.pdf. [3]

IARD (2018), *Alcohol in the Shadow Economy: Unregulated, Untaxed, and Potentially Toxic*, International Alliance for Responsible Drinking, http://www.iard.org/getattachment/1b56787b-cc6d-4ebb-989f-6684cf1df624/alcohol-in-the-shadow-economy.pdf. [6]

IARD (2018), *Alcohol in the Shadow Economy: Unregulated, Untaxed, and Potentially Toxic*, International Alliance for Responsible Drinking, http://www.iard.org/getattachment/1b56787b-cc6d-4ebb-989f-6684cf1df624/alcohol-in-the-shadow-economy.pdf. [4]

International, E. (ed.) (2018), *Análisis del Mercado Ilegal de Bebidas Alcohólicas en Paraguay*, http://www.tracit.org/uploads/1/0/2/2/102238034/cervepar_illegal_alcohol_in_paraguay__final_2018.pdf. [15]

International, E. (ed.) (2018), *Market Analysis for Illicit Alcohol in Sub-Saharan Africa*, http://www.tracit.org/uploads/1/0/2/2/102238034/illicit_alcohol_trade__africa_sub_saharan_africa_pan__regional_report_final_14_sep_2018.pdf. [10]

Lachenmeier Dirk W. Maria Neufeld and Jürgen Rehm (2021), *The Impact of Unrecorded Alcohol Use on Health: What Do We Know in 2020?*, Journal of Studies on Alcohol and Drugs, https://doi.org/10.15288/jsad.2021.82.28. [2]

OECD/EUIPO (2021b), *Global Trade in Fakes: a Worrying Threat*, OECD Publishing, https://www.oecd.org/publications/global-trade-in-fakes-74c81154-en.htm. [7]

Probst Charlotte et al. (2019), *The global proportion and volume of unrecorded alcohol in 2015*, Journal of Global Health, Edinburgh, http://www.jogh.org/documents/issue201901/jogh-09-010421.pdf. [1]

Notes

1 See WHO. (2010). WHO Global Strategy to reduce the harmful uses of alcohol. Geneva: WHO. Section 37. Available at: https://www.who.int/publications/i/item/9789241599931.

2 See Manning, L., & Kowalska, A. (2021). Illicit alcohol: Public health risk of methanol poisoning and policy mitigation strategies. Foods, 10(7), 1625. and Lachenmeier, D. W. (2012). Unrecorded and illicit alcohol. 2012) Alcohol in the European Union. Consumption, harm and policy approaches, 29-34.

3 See (OECD/EUIPO, 2021b[7]), Global Trade in Fakes: A Worrying Threat, Illicit Trade, OECD Publishing, Paris, https://doi.org/10.1787/74c81154-en.

4 Euromonitor has also conducted country studies on Argentina (Euromonitor, 2014[19]), Bolivia (Euromonitor, 2017[18]), Colombia, Ecuador, El Salvador, Honduras, Panama and Peru (Euromonitor, 2016[9]) and (Euromonitor, 2016[8]), Czech Republic (Euromonitor, 2015[14]) Dominican Republic (Euromonitor, 2017[13]), Guatemala (Euromonitor, 2016[17]), Malawi (Euromonitor, 2016[11]), Mexico (Euromonitor, 2018[16]), Paraguay (Euromonitor, 2018[15]), Russia (Euromonitor, 2015[12]) and Sub-Saharan Africa (Euromonitor, 2018[10]).

5 Existing actions to combat illicit trade

This chapter illustrates how governments, businesses and civil society have responded to the challenges posed by illicit alcohol trade in various ways, some of which are discussed in the section on the effects of the pandemic on the markets for illicit alcohol. There is also a summary of some other key actions taken at the governmental and intergovernmental levels, and by other key players.

Country policies designed to address illicit trade

At the governmental level, the WHO reports that some 80 countries (more than half of the 165+ reporting jurisdictions) have written national alcohol policies (WHO, 2018[1]), Most national policies include provisions that address informal or illicit production of beer and wine (79%) and spirits (84%). In addition, 81% have a national policy regarding sales of informal or illicit beer, while 84% have such a policy for wine sales, and 88% have a policy that applies to sales of spirits. In the case of the United Kingdom, the country has developed a standalone alcohol policy that aims at enhancing efforts to combat fraud, while improving and strengthening tax collection mechanisms (HM Revenue & Customs, 2016[2]); the strategy complements the country's overall alcohol strategy, which contains related provisions, albeit to a lesser extent (HM Government, 2012[3]).

However, although illicit alcohol may be addressed in national policies, enforcement is poor in many countries, particularly lower-income countries where the illicit alcohol market is large. Many countries that do not have national policies nonetheless have national legislation governing the production and sale of informal and illicit alcohol. In all, more than 118 countries surveyed have legislation governing the production of unrecorded alcohol, while more than 125 countries have legislation covering the sale of the illicit or informal products. A large number of countries (144) reported having a system to track informally produced and illicit alcohol. The most common methods for the tracking were police investigations (121 responding countries), complaint systems (83 countries) and case-by-case reporting (80 countries). Active surveillance (67 responding countries) and tracking by the liquor licensing authority (66 countries) were also used in some jurisdictions.

Intergovernmental work on enforcement

At the intergovernmental level, actions have been taken by INTERPOL and Europol to disrupt illicit trade globally.

INTERPOL-Europol

INTERPOL and Europol launched Operation OPSON in 2011 as a joint operation targeting counterfeit and substandard food and beverages. It initially involved the participation of 9 EU countries, plus Turkey.[1] Its original principal objectives were to i) raise awareness of the dangers posed by counterfeit and substandard food and drink, ii) establish partnerships with the private sector to provide a cohesive response to this type of crime and iii) protect consumers by seizing and destroying substandard foods and identifying the actors behind these networks. These objectives have since been further elaborated over time and now include i) protecting public health, ii) fighting against organized crime groups involved in the trade of fake and substandard food, iii) enhancing international co-operation, iv) enhancing national co-operation between local enforcement agencies and food regulatory agencies, and v) enhancing co-operation with private partners from the food and beverage industry.

The OPSON operations have been carried out regularly, with a growing number of countries taking part. The most recent campaign, OPSON X, took place between December 2020 and July 2021, with the participation of some 72 countries.[2] The operation netted 15,451 tonnes of illegal products, with an estimated street value of EUR 53.8 million. Nearly 68 000 checks were carried out, resulting in more than 1 000 criminal cases being opened. The enforcement actions uncovered new leads for future investigations. More than 600 arrest warrants were issued, resulting in the disruption in the activities of about 42 organized crime groups around the world. The most seized goods in were alcohol and food supplements, followed by cereals and grain products. Alcoholic drinks were the products that were most commonly counterfeited.

A more comprehensive assessment was published on the OSON IX campaign, which took place between 1 December 2019 and 15 June 2020 (INTERPOL/Europol, 2021[4]). Some 77 countries, including six G7 countries (Canada, France Germany, Italy, the United Kingdom and the United States), participated in the campaign. The countries carried out checks throughout their national territory, focusing on the whole chain of supply. Seizures being made at production sites, during the transport phase or at the distribution and selling points of illicit foods and drinks. All channels of distribution, including online sales, were covered. The operation resulted in:

- the seizure of 12 000 tonnes of products, valued at USD 40 million (of which alcoholic beverages was the leading good seized, at USD 5.8 million); and
- the disruption in the operations of 19 organised crime groups, 407 arrest warrants, the execution of 235 search warrants, 408 criminal cases and 2 980 administrative cases.

The number of checks were about 39 per cent of what the countries reported in OPSON VIII, while criminal cases were 13 per cent of the OPSON VIII level, most likely reflecting the effects of COVID-19 on operations.

The operation confirmed that alcohol is a highly targeted product for smuggling, adulteration and counterfeiting, and, in terms of food crime, it continues to be one of the main global threats to the health and life of the consumers, and also to the revenues of state budgets (Box 5.1). Alcoholic beverages were, in fact, the second most seized commodity in OPSON IX, totalling about 1 613 tonnes of products. Of the total seized, almost 1 300 tonnes were wine. The other types of alcohol present in higher quantities amongst seizures were vodka and whiskey respectively. Countries which reported notable seizures in this regard were France with more than one million litres of wine, Italy with more than 45 000 litres of wine in two large seizures, Portugal with 21 000 litres of wine in one seizure, Greece with more than 70 000 litres of wine, ethyl alcohol and whiskey in five large seizures and Spain with one large seizure of 18 000 litres of wine. In all other cases the average volume of alcohol seized was about 94 litres per seizure. In total, 54 arrests, 31 search warrants and 4 organised criminal groups (OCGs) were reported in connection with this illicit commodity and the total value of the goods seized is around USD 20.3 million.

Box 5.1. Examples of seizures of alcohol in OPSON VIII and IX campaigns

Albania.-- Some 8 000 litres of wine valued at USD 20 000 were seized as the goods, which originated in Italy, lacked proof of customs declaration. Two arrest warrants were issued.

Belarus.-- Belarusian nationals were found to be transporting alcohol in bottles or cans without excise stamps, using personal vehicles, minivans or trucks. The alcohol was intended for local markets and/or possibly for transit to neighboring countries. In total, more than 14 000 litres of illicit alcohol were seized.

Eswatini.-- Border controls revealed counterfeit alcohol, especially whiskey and vodka, and counterfeit condiments. In all cases, the actors involved were local persons, with international connections.

Greece.-- One case involved an OCG importing alcoholic beverages and raw materials (ethyl alcohol) for the production of the fake spirits for the domestic market. The spirits were bottled with forged brand name labels, and then distributed as genuine products to liquor stores, grocery shops, bars and night clubs. The OCG used international transport trucks vehicles to import illegal alcoholic beverages, comingling them with genuine products, in order not to be easily detected by the LEA. One subgroup of the OCG was primarily responsible for the storage of the products and replacing foreign labels with fake Greek logos. The fake products were then sold as Greek products with virtual invoices with the OCG gaining large profits from the differences in the taxes imposed. A second subgroup was responsible for the production, storage and distribution of the substandard alcohol. In support of their illegal activities, the OCG had set up two fully equipped laboratories and four warehouses in Attica. On

---

20th of February 2020, a police operation was carried out, which resulted in the arrest of 14 individuals, including a top OCG operative, and the seizure of 21 901 bottles of alcoholic beverages and 22 500 litres of raw materials (ethyl alcohol).

Italy.-- Operation "Vuoti a rendere", which was launched in January 2018, in the framework of OPSON VII and finalized during OPSON IX, focused on Italian counterfeiters responsible for food fraud, including the counterfeiting of prestigious wines. The investigation revealed a fraud based on the reuse of original primary packaging (empty wine bottles) and secondary packaging (wooden boxes). The bottles were refilled with cheap products from different origins, purchased online or at discount stores. Packaging films and false masking guarantee seals were applied to conceal the lack of distinctive signs on the capsules used for the counterfeit units. Once a contact with a buyer was established via e-commerce, the counterfeiters further increased their promotional offers, setting prices significantly below the market price for genuine products.

The Italian police, supported by Europol, took down the network of wine counterfeiters with raids in eight Italian provinces. Following the raids, an illegal storehouse, where the refilling activity was being performed, was found. Eleven individuals were referred to the Judicial Authority for participation in wine counterfeiting and food fraud. Close to 1 200 bottles were seized, the most expensive of which a Bordeaux wine worth EUR 4 200.00.

Russian Federation.-- The police dismantled an underground facility used for producing alcoholic beverages. The laboratory analysis showed that the products were substandard, lacking the physico-chemical parameters required, thereby posing a threat to public health.

South Africa.-- Authorities seized more than 6 000 litres of traditional Asian alcoholic beverages, which were transported by sea containers for illegal importation into the country. In another operation, dismantling of a counterfeiting network resulted in the arrest of 2 Chinese and 1 Mozambique traders. The silver caps on the alcohol bottles marking the products for export were replaced with counterfeit ones, in order to hide the origin of the products and their intended destination. After switching the caps, the products were distributed in South Africa, with the perpetrators pocketing significant sums via tax evasion.

Finally, South African authorities intercepted a consignment of imported counterfeit labels, which arrived by air. Authorities raided the final destination premises, finding large quantities of counterfeit labels and alcohol, which was to be relabeled for sale in the domestic market. Six Chinese national were arrested and equipment, unused labels and alcohol were seized.

Source: (INTERPOL/Europol, 2020[5]) and (INTERPOL/Europol, 2021[4]).

The 12 000, tonnes of seizures in OPSON IX were significantly lower than in OPSON VIII, which were at record levels, with seizures of 33 000 tonnes (valued at about USD 59 million). Alcoholic beverages were the most seized product in that operation; they were reported in 633 cases, by 23 countries (INTERPOL/Europol, 2020[5]) and (INTERPOL/Europol, 2021[4]). In OPSON VIII, a total of 433 arrests and 423 searches were recorded, with LEAs disrupting 34 organized crime groups (OCGs), of which 15 were directly involved in the production or distribution of counterfeit products. Twelve persons were prosecuted and 433 persons were identified as suspects for involvement in illicit deeds involving alcoholic beverages.

The report on OPSON IX further confirmed a previous trend relating to alcohol smuggling from Eastern European countries to the European Union, namely, frequent shipping of small quantities of the products (INTERPOL/Europol, 2021[4]). With respect to the nature of the illicit activities, intellectual property right (IPR) violations accounted for 8.5% of the seizures, for those cases where the type of infringement was reported. The report on OPSON VIII provides more detail in this regard (INTERPOL, Europol, 2020). In that campaign, seizures of products that were designed to deceive consumers accounted for 88% of the volume of products seized (but only 2% of the number of reports). Seizures of products associated with fiscal fraud, on the other hand, was present in 66% of the reports on seizures (but only 1% of the volume of products seized. Thus large quantities of products that were designed to deceive consumers were seized in a handful of cases, while small quantities of products involving fiscal fraud were seized in a large number of cases. With respect to counterfeiting, 6.5% of reports were linked to counterfeit products (0.13% by quantity).

Looking forward, the report on OPSON IX calls for increasing international co-operation in exchanging reliable operational information, which is essential in understanding new developments and the real impact that the pandemic is having on the global food chain security. The disruption caused by the pandemic showed that opportunistic crime is ready to take advantage of the vulnerabilities of the regional and global supply chains; contingency planning is viewed as of crucial importance in order for LEAs to respond in a timely manner. It is further recommended that Operation OPSON remain global, with, however, a more pronounced regional focus. To this end, it is recommended that member countries ask for or participate in regional case meetings organized by INTERPOL and Europol, taking full advantage of tools for organizing virtual meetings.

Private partners have been invited to support the operation based on their presence in the different markets (Europe, USA, Middle East, Africa, South America, Asia), prioritizing those most affected by the threat of counterfeiting. Their participation was made on a voluntary basis and did not imply any specific action from the law enforcement agencies. The participation of the private partners consisted of:

- Providing intelligence and risk assessments on their products during the pre-operational phase, including during training sessions tailored for law enforcement services;
- Participating in preparatory meetings organized at the national level; and
- Providing expertise in legal proceedings when needed.

In OPSON VIII, twenty-two private partners took part, including 8 companies or associations representing the interests of alcoholic beverage producers (INTERPOL/Europol, 2020[5]).

WCO

As indicated earlier, illicit trade in alcohol is a major concern of customs authorities, and the WCO, working with its member countries, is actively engaged in activities to disrupt the illegal trade. In response to the growing danger posed by illicit trade in alcohol, Project SHOT was launched in 2016 to monitor global trends in alcohol fraud (WCO, 2019[6]) and (WCO, 2021[7]). The primary objectives of the project are to:

- Exchange information on alcohol seizures among the 183 WCO Member States within the 11 Regional Intelligence Liaison Offices (RILO);
- Produce a report reviewing alcohol-smuggling activities covering all the geographical regions of the existing 11 RILOs;
- Improve the quantity and quality of data incorporated into the Customs Enforcement Network (CEN) system;
- Improve the quality of the common analytical products;
- Promote co-operation within the RILO Network; and
- Identify areas of risk.

Initially, the project was foreseen for the first half of 2017, but it was later extended through 2020 (WCO, 2021[7]). The project focuses on the illicit turnover of both genuine and counterfeit alcohol, as well as information on seizures of machinery and components utilized in the illegal production of alcohol. Additionally, cases involving illegal alcohol factories are considered (WCO, 2019[6]).

Involvement in the operations has increased over time, rising from 42 countries (in 7 RILOs) in 2018, to 58 countries (in 11 RILOs) in 2019. The countries taking part reported on 4,726 cases, in which 37.3 million litres of alcohol were seized, in 2019. Saudi Arabia and Ireland together accounted for close to 60% of the total cases reported, with no other country accounting for more than 7% of the total (WCO, 2021[7]). Land borders were involved in more than half the cases (52.2%), followed by seaports (27%), inland (11.4%) and airports (7.6%).

WCO-INTERPOL

On 23-27 July 2012, WCO and INTERPOL carried out a joint operation against illicit trafficking in Africa. [3] Operation Meerkat saw customs and police authorities carry out some 40 raids at seaports, inland border crossing points, markets and shops in Angola, Kenya, Mozambique, Namibia, South Africa, Tanzania and Zimbabwe. More than 32 million cigarettes, 134 tonnes of raw tobacco and almost 3 000 litres of alcohol were seized, resulting in national authorities initiating a number of administrative investigations into tax evasion and other potential criminal offences.

WHO

The work of the World Health Organization (WHO) on alcohol has included significant attention to the challenges posed by unrecorded products, much of which is illicit. In 2010, the WHO, in consultation with stakeholders, developed a *Global strategy to reduce the harmful use of alcohol* (WHO, 2010[8]). One of the 10 policy areas identified for action concerned measures that could be taken to reduce the public health impact of illicit alcohol and informally produced alcohol. The report notes the importance of addressing the health risks posed by illicit and informal alcohol due to their higher ethanol content and potential contamination with toxic substances, such as methanol. It also notes that the illicit and informal products could also hamper governments' abilities to tax and control legally produced alcohol. Recommended policy interventions were six-fold:

- establishing good quality control with regard to production and distribution of alcoholic beverages;
- regulating sales of informally produced alcohol and bringing it into the taxation system;
- establishing an efficient control and enforcement system;
- developing or strengthening tracking and tracing systems for illicit alcohol;
- ensuring necessary co-operation and exchange of relevant information on combating illicit alcohol among authorities at national and international levels; and
- issuing relevant public warnings about contaminants and other health threats from informal or illicit alcohol.

At the same time, in its *Handbook for action to reduce alcohol-related harm* (WHO, 2019[9]), the WHO recommends that consideration be given to undercutting the market for illicit alcohol, by adopting government efforts to control these markets and tax policies that make lower-alcohol forms of culturally preferred beverages more accessible to consumers.

A follow-up draft report on *Global alcohol action plan 2022-2030 to strengthen implementation of the Global Strategy to Reduce the Harmful Use of Alcohol*, notes that limited progress had been made in developing and implementing strategies in countries (WHO, 2021[10]). In the case of illicit alcohol, the report further notes that the capacity of governments to deal with illicit production, distribution and consumption of alcohol, including safety issues, is limited or inadequate, particularly in jurisdictions where unrecorded alcohol makes up a significant proportion of all alcohol consumed.

The report cites the need for research on the consumption of informally and illegally produced alcohol and its health consequences and sets out an action plan for boosting the effective implementation of the global strategy during 2022-30. This includes a proposal to develop and support the implementation of activities for reducing the public health impact of illicitly or informally produced alcohol, taking into consideration the differences in strategies to address informally and illegally produced alcohol, including activities related to the assessment of the level of unrecorded alcohol consumption in populations, the efficient control of alcohol production and distribution, raising awareness of the associated health risks and community mobilization.

A submission by industry to WHO on the draft action plan recommends that consideration be given to inclusion of measures that control alcohol markets without stimulating demand for illicit products and the consequential health risks associated with illicit products. The recommended measures include:

- Regulating and controlling the supply of raw materials, particularly ethanol.
- Monitoring production sites and requiring health and sanitary permits for manufacturers.
- Strengthening national borders and law enforcement departments to identify and prevent illicit activity.
- Strengthening penalties for illicit activity to increase their deterrent effect.
- Improving a country's overall business environment to encourage businesses to operate legitimately.
- Raising level of awareness of the threat of the illicit trade and its consequences.

Industry stakeholders

A number of private stakeholders have been addressing issues concerning illicit alcohol trade and have developed policy recommendations and tools to this end. These include the International Alliance for Responsible Drinking (IARD) and the Transnational Alliance to Combat Illicit Trade (TRACIT).

IARD

The IARD, in which 13 leading producers of wine, beer and spirits participate, has conducted considerable work on unrecorded and illicit alcohol. This includes case studies on the situation in the Baltic States (IARD, 2018[11]), Botswana (IARD, 2018[12]), India (IARD, 2018[13]) and Vietnam (IARD, 2018[14]), as well as a report on the situation with non-commercial alcohol in nine countries (Belarus, Botswana, Brazil, China, India, Kenya, Mexico, Russia, and Sri Lanka) (IARD, 2012[15]). Additional reports include an assessment of the situation worldwide, with recommendations for the actions that stakeholders should take to address the situation (see Annex A) (IARD, 2018[16]), and a policy brief.[4]

The organisation's work also includes the development of an online toolkit[5] for assessing the scope of the unrecorded alcohol market, the aim of which is to:

- serve as a resource for those interested in gaining a better understanding of the issue of unrecorded alcohol;
- provide a menu of approaches that can be used to investigate the unrecorded alcohol market, depending on the research question, context, and existing data and resources available; and
- provide a road map for achieving, to the greatest extent possible, consistency and uniformity across studies so that results can be compared in a sound manner.

On the policy front, in recognition of the growing role of e-commerce in alcohol market, the organisation entered into partnership with 12 (now 14) major global and regional online retailers and ecommerce and delivery platforms operating in six continents, to work on establishing global standards for improved policing of the online sale and delivery of alcohol beverages.6 The partnership, which was announced in January 2021, resulted in the issuance of standards in May (IARD, 2021[17]). The standards are aimed at:

- verifying that sales are made to parties meeting the legal purchase age;

- preventing delivery to those who are underaged, intoxicated, or where delivery is prohibited by law;
- providing training tools, information, and education for drivers;
- enhancing consumer information and control; and
- putting in place effective monitoring of the situation.

TRACIT

The Transnational Alliance to Combat Illicit Trade (TRACIT) is an organisation which is actively involved in i) analysing illicit trade, with specific attention to alcohol and ii) proposing actions to combat illegal activities (Box 5.2). Its member companies encompass 1 500 global brands and subsidiaries, which operate in 190 countries. Work on alcohol includes country reports on Costa Rica (TRACIT, 2019[18]), India (TRACIT, 2019[19]) and South Africa (TRACIT, 2019[20]). The organisation has also done related work on the impact that illicit trade can have on sustainable development goals, with specific reference to the situation of illicit alcohol (TRACIT, 2019[21]) and (TRACIT, 2021[22]) and has assessed the effects of the pandemic on illicit trade in alcohol (TRACIT, 2021[23]).

Box 5.2. TRACIT policy recommendations

Governments employ a variety of regulatory and legal mechanisms to control harmful consumption of alcohol and to combat illicit alcohol, with differing degrees of success. Many frameworks are ineffectively designed, offer only partial solutions, or are inadequately enforced or resourced. Some mechanisms may even unintentionally boost illicit alcohol consumption by making it more difficult for consumers to access or afford licit beverages. TRACIT recommends that governments consider a portfolio of recognized policy and regulatory controls that can help control illicit alcohol:

Raise awareness of illicit alcohol, particularly at the grassroots level with emphasis on the severe health risks associated with consumption of illicit alcohol. Awareness campaigns should educate consumers the negative economic impacts, such as lost tax revenues that could have been invested in schools, roads or other much needed infrastructure. Consumers should also be educated on how they are likely aiding criminal organisations when they buy illicit alcohol. Moreover, awareness campaigns must also consider the harmful drinking patterns that are associated with consumption of unrecorded alcohol.

Improve accessibility of legal products at affordable prices and increase the density of legal outlets to stem demand for illicit products. Increasing the number of legal retail outlets that sell legitimate alcohol is an effective way to curb the sale of illicit alcohol. Effective monitoring of retail outlets is also crucial to ensure that these units do not trade in illicit alcohol. Strategies that seek to effectively regulate the commercial availability of alcohol are also important ways to reduce the general level of harmful use of alcohol. This is especially true in rural areas where the density of shops is particularly low and the ease of access to unregulated alcohol is high.

Enforce laws and impose sanctions and penalties at levels sufficient to deter criminal activity. Effective enforcement of laws requires co-ordination among border countries, national government agencies (revenue, border, police, health, etc.) and different levels of government. Moreover, imposing administrative, criminal and civil penalties for illicit trade in alcohol should be a priority to prohibit illicit traders from exploiting markets with the weakest penal regimes. Consideration must also be given to rescinding business licenses from retailers, manufacturers and distributors involved in illegal trade. As contraband beverages such as whiskey and vodka are the most common form of illicit alcohol, it is necessary to assess more carefully their origin.

Rationalize tax policies and subsidies to ensure that they do not incentivize illicit trade, smuggling, adulteration and theft. Tax policies need to account for various demand-related factors including overall consumption, price, income levels and the ensuing affordability of products.

Control the production and importation of ethanol. Countries with very low levels of counterfeit alcohol have effective systems in place to control the trade of ethanol. Ethanol meant for non-consumption purposes (such as pharmacy alcohol, beauty and personal care products, and industrial use) should be denatured and is not levied excise tax. Countries such as Colombia and Peru have new legislation in place to control the ethanol market. These efforts have achieved positive results in controlling the flow of local and smuggled ethanol diverted to the illicit market to produce illicit distilled beverages.

Promote the creation of local private-public partnerships to bring key industry and government stakeholders together to define strategies including: developing and deploying technology solutions based on internationally recognized open standards to protect the integrity of products and supply chains; ensure easy sharing of intelligence and data to improve risk assessment and border control; improving awareness; expanding the knowledge base; and finding new ways to tell apart legal from illicit beverages.

Multi-sector engagement is necessary because no one sector by itself can address the complexities of illicit trade. Like endeavours in other areas, efforts to reduce the harmful effects of alcohol and reduction of illicit alcohol can benefit from working together.

In addition to the above, there are a number of other international organisations that are active in specifically combatting illicit trade in alcohol. The *Alliance Against Counterfeit Spirits* (AACS) represents the world's major international spirits producing companies.[7] The organisation, which has been in operation since the early 1990s, has been actively engaged in the training of law enforcement officials, and in supporting enforcement actions, which have resulted in the seizure of millions of counterfeit bottles, caps and labels. One of the principal objectives of the *World Spirits Alliance*, which was formed in 2019 with the participation of producers of spirits worldwide, is to support the development of ambitious strategies to combat illicit alcohol.[8]

The World Wine Trade Group (WWTG) is an informal grouping of governments and industry representatives from wine-producing countries that address wine-related matters affecting the wine trade: Argentina, Australia, Canada, Chile, Georgia, New Zealand, the United States, and South Africa. Founded in 1998, the Group aims to facilitate international trade in wine through information sharing, discussion of regulatory issues in wine markets, and joint actions for the removal of trade barriers. The WWTG has negotiated three agreements and one MOU that promote international wine trade, including a 2017 *Arrangement on Information Exchange, Technical Cooperation and Counterfeiting.*[9,10]

References

HM Government (2012), *The Government's Alcohol Strategy*, Home Office, [3]
https://assets.publishing.service.gov.uk/government/uploads/system/uploads/attachment_dat
a/file/224075/alcohol-strategy.pdf.

HM Revenue & Customs (2016), *The HMRC Alcohol Strategy: Modernising alcohol taxes to tackle fraud and reduce burdens on alcohol businesses*, HM Revenue & Customs, https://assets.publishing.service.gov.uk/government/uploads/system/uploads/attachment_data/file/510235/HMRC_Alcohol_Strategy.pdf. [2]

IARD (2021), *Global standards for online alcohol sales and delivery*, International Alliance for Responsible Drinking, http://www.iard.org/IARD/media/Documents/25052021-Global-standards-for-online-alcohol-sale-and-delivery.pdf. [17]

IARD (2018), *Alcohol in the Shadow Economy: Unregulated, Untaxed, and Potentially Toxic*, International Alliance for Responsible Drinking, http://www.iard.org/getattachment/1b56787b-cc6d-4ebb-989f-6684cf1df624/alcohol-in-the-shadow-economy.pdf. [16]

IARD (2018), *Unrecorded Alcohol in Botswana: Results of a Population Survey*, International Alliance for Responsible Drinking, http://www.iard.org/getattachment/6c1e77ed-7964-4ab5-83bc-366cee06b1e0/botswana-alcohol-consumer-survey-final-report-08mar17-rev-08dec18.pdf. [12]

IARD (2018), *Unrecorded Alcohol in India: Results of a Population Survey in Five States*, International Alliance for Responsible Drinking, http://www.iard.org/getattachment/fdd90791-41cb-4bd3-98f0-555fbf9818f8/unrecorded-alcohol-in-india.pdf. [13]

IARD (2018), *Unrecorded Alcohol in the Baltic States: Results of a Population Survey*, International Alliance for Responsible Drinking, http://www.iard.org/getattachment/36c0ecba-1ae2-4d53-9b9a-97cd9c0357b3/sura-baltics-summary-report.pdf. [11]

IARD (2018), *Unrecorded Alcohol in Vietnam: Results of a Population Survey*, International Alliance for Responsible Drinking. Report in Vietnamese available at, http://www.iard.org/getattachment/0d62ac14-4046-44ea-a472-f0ca7dd2d686/ipss_consumptionofalcoholbeveragesinvietnam.pdf. [14]

IARD (2012), *Producers, sellers, and drinkers - Studies of noncommercial alcohol in nine countries*, International Alliance for Responsible Drinking, http://www.iard.org/getattachment/9725694a-dbdb-4f27-b581-5211004e0b3c/icap-producers-sellers-and-drinkers-noncommercial-alcohol-monograph.pdf. [15]

INTERPOL/Europol (2021), *Operation OPSON IX: Analysis Report*, http://www.europol.europa.eu/sites/default/files/documents/opson_ix_report_2021_0.pdf. [4]

INTERPOL/Europol (2020), *Operation OPSON VIII: Analysis Report*, http://www.europol.europa.eu/sites/default/files/documents/opson_viii_report_public_version.pdf. [5]

TRACIT (2021), *Mapping the Effects of Illicit Trade on the Sustainable Development Goals*, Transnational Alliance to Combat Illicit Trade, http://www.tracit.org/uploads/1/0/2/2/102238034/tracit_examining_the_negative_impacts_of_illicit_trade_on_sdg_16.pdf. [22]

TRACIT (2021), *Prohibition, Illicit Alcohol and Lessons Learned from Lockdown*, Transnational Alliance to Combat Illicit Trade, https://www.tracit.org/uploads/1/0/2/2/102238034/tracit_prohibition_illicit_alcohol_and_lessons_learned_from_lockdown_jan2021_hr.pdf. [23]

TRACIT (2019), *Illicit Trade in Alcohol in Costa Rica: Challenges and Solutions*, Transnational Alliance to Combat Illicit Trade, http://www.tracit.org/uploads/1/0/2/2/102238034/tracit-illicit_trade_in_alcohol-challenges_and_solutions_final_english.pdf. [18]

TRACIT (2019), *Illicit Trade in Alcohol in India: Challenges and Solutions*, Transnational Alliance to Combat Illicit Trade, https://www.tracit.org/uploads/1/0/2/2/102238034/tracit_-_india_alcohol_report_-_master_copy-_september_2019.pdf. [19]

TRACIT (2019), *Illicit Trade in Alcohol in South Africa: Challenges and Solutions*, Transnational Alliance to Combat Illicit Trade, http://www.tracit.org/uploads/1/0/2/2/102238034/tracit_south_africa_report_and_recommendations.pdf. [20]

TRACIT (2019), *Mapping the Impact of Illicit Trade on the Sustainable Development Goals, Transnational Alliance to Combat Illicit Trade*, https://unctad.org/system/files/non-official-document/DITC2019_TRACIT_IllicitTradeandSDGs_fullreport_en. [21]

WCO (2021), *Project SHOT, Presentation at the OECD TF-CIT webinar on "Crisis policy, illicit alcohol and lessons learned from lockdown"*, unpublished. [7]

WCO (2019), *Illicit Trade Report 2018*, World Customs Organization, Brussels, http://www.wcoomd.org/-/media/wco/public/global/pdf/topics/enforcement-and-compliance/activities-and-programmes/illicit-trade-report/itr_2018_en.pdf?db=web. [6]

WHO (2021), *Global alcohol action plan 2022-2030 to strengthen implementation of the Global Strategy to Reduce the Harmful Use of Alcohol,*, World Health Organization, Geneva, http://www.who.int/publications/m/item/global-action-plan-on-alcohol-1st-draft. [10]

WHO (2019), *Handbook for action to reduce alcohol-related harm*, World Health Organization, Regional Operations for Europe, Copenhagen, http://www.euro.who.int/__data/assets/pdf_file/0012/43320/E92820.pdf. [9]

WHO (2018), *Global status report on alcohol and health*, World Health Organization, Geneva, https://apps.who.int/iris/rest/bitstreams/1151838/retrieve. [1]

WHO (2010), *Global strategy to reduce the harmful use of alcohol*, World Health Organization, Geneva, http://www.afro.who.int/sites/default/files/2017-06/9789241599931_eng.pdf. [8]

Notes

[1] See www.europol.europa.eu/newsroom/news/tonnes-of-illicit-foods-seized-across-europe-in-interpol-europol-led-operation.

[2] See www.interpol.int/en/News-and-Events/News/2021/Illicit-food-and-drink-worth-EUR-53-million-seized-in-global-operation.

[3] See www.wcoomd.org/en/media/newsroom/2012/august/wco-and-interpol-joint-operation-against-illicit-trafficking-in-africa-leads-to-tobacco-and-alcohol-seizures.

[4] See www.iard.org/getattachment/d76b085b-6a26-4080-b846-ca5df14e301e/pr-unrecorded.pdf.

[5] See http://iardunrecordedtoolkit.org/home.

[6] See www.iard.org/IARD/media/Documents/29012021-E-commerce-partnership-announcement.pdf. The global and regional online retailers and ecommerce and delivery platforms include Coles (Australia), Cornershop (Canada, Latin America, United Sates), Drizly (United States), Endeavour Group (Australia), Glovo (Africa, Europe, Latin America, Middle East), Grab (Southeast Asia), , HipBar (India), JD.com (China), Jumia (Africa), Minibar Delivery (United States), Mercado Libre (Latin America), Retail Drinks Australia (Australia), ReserveBar (United States) and Uber Eats (six continents).

[7] See https://aacs-global.com/.

[8] See www.worldspiritsalliance.com/.

[9] See https://legacy.trade.gov/td/ocg/wwtg.htm and/www.wwtg-gmcv.org/

[10] See https://legacy.trade.gov/td/ocg/2017WWTGArrangement.pdf

6 Conclusions

The analysis summarised in this report highlights that the market for illicit alcohol is a large one and attractive to illicit traders for at least three reasons.

- First, illicit products are relatively easy to produce and consumers can be easily deceived. The large premium carried by branded products translates into potentially high profits for illicit traders of illicit, counterfeit items, which make them an area of great interest. While penalties for counterfeiting can be high, the persistence of counterfeiting worldwide suggest that illicit traders view the risk of detection and prosecution as acceptable.

- Second, governments have imposed significant taxes on alcohol, to raise revenue and/or to discourage particular behaviour or purchase. While taxes on alcohol have also proven to be an important source of revenue to governments, one of the main factors driving illicit sales in alcoholic beverages is price differential between illicit and licit alcohol that is linked to the differences in taxes and tariffs imposed on various alcoholic products across countries. This situation can create incentives for entrepreneurial parties to avoid them i) by smuggling product from low-taxed areas to higher-taxed ones and ii) by producing products clandestinely so as to avoid taxes. As the products being smuggled are legitimate, they do not have to be tampered with, which simplifies the illicit operations. The principal challenge for the illicit traders is mainly to be effective in concealing their smuggling, which does not appear to be a significant barrier as much of the smuggling is carried out through road transport, which offers significant opportunities for avoiding detection. As with counterfeiting, the penalties for smuggling and tax fraud can be high, but illicit traders appear to be generally undeterred as such activities continue to test enforcement authorities worldwide.

- Third, illicit traders can become involved in the unauthorised manufacture of alcohol. The cost of producing illicit spirits products can be quite low in small scale operations, which means the market is relatively open to small- and large-scale operators alike. The illicit traders can focus on producing and selling low-cost alternatives to branded products, or they can try to market their illicit production as higher quality, branded products. In both cases, the producers will be tempted to run their operations with a view towards minimising costs, resulting in the use of ingredients that could endanger consumer well-being, resulting, in some instances, in death.

One of the principal challenges for large volume illicit traders is in infiltrating supply chains, which are highly regulated in most countries. Success in this regard undoubtedly relies on the lack of awareness and in some cases complicity of distributors, off-premises retailers, and on-premises establishments. E-commerce, however, is rapidly increasing its role in distribution, which is a phenomenon warranting attention as it affords illicit traders with, from their perspective, a very promising channel for expanding sales.

Of particular concern in the above is the role of organised crime, which is a primary driver of illicit operations. The success that they have had comes at the cost of legitimate producers in the case of counterfeit and low-cost unbranded items, and at the cost of governments as a result of uncollected taxes. Moreover, the substantial proceeds of illicit sales are used to fund other illegal activities, empowering criminal organisations while undermining the rule of law in counties and trust in public institutions.

There are also significant health risks associated with illicit trade in alcohol. In general, the biggest health concern is consumer exposure to health risks associated with toxic illicit alternatives. Beyond the fact that these illicit substitutes do not comply with sanitary, quality and safety regulations, the most hazardous are contaminated with toxic, lethal chemicals. According to WHO, it is important to promote policies that reduce harmful consumption of alcohol – and illicit alcohol is regarded as the worst form of harmful alcohol consumption.

Policy areas for stakeholders' consideration

The analysis of markets for illicit trade in alcohol presented in this report, lends itself to formulate some policy areas for stakeholders' consideration:

Improving information. Much of the information on illicit alcohol trade reported by governments is anecdotal in nature, with some notable exceptions, such as reports prepared by INTERPOL and Europol. Beyond this, the private sector has contributed significant research to measure the size, shape and drivers of the illicit trade in alcohol. Nonetheless, more reporting by a greater number of stakeholders would help improve the quality and quantity of information needed by policy makers to make informed decisions. In cases of physical harm from consuming illicit alcohol, improved information sharing could include effective alert systems for notifying stakeholders across jurisdictions of important developments.

Addressing the issue of online alcohol sales. At the same time, more attention needs to be paid to the growing use of online platforms to sell alcohol, which have been used to sell illicit products.

Formulating comprehensive alcohol strategies to combat illicit trade. Most countries have national alcohol policies. Given the significant levels of illicit alcohol that already exist—and the significant negative impact on society and economy—such policies should necessarily also include provisions to address illicit alcohol. The link between alcohol policies and the illicit trade is essential and alcohol policies should not be developed in isolation from realities of the local market. For instance, attention should be given to the different types and methods in which illicit alcohol products (spirits, wine and beer) are traded and the proportionality between the effectiveness of potentially curbing illicit trade, the cost of the remedy and the potential disruption to legitimate business. Considering objectives to reduce alcohol-related harm, the World Health Organisation (WHO) recommends undercutting the market for illicit alcohol, through government efforts to control these markets and tax policies that make lower-alcohol forms of culturally preferred beverages more accessible to consumers. There may be value in elaborating more comprehensive standalone policies that focus on strengthening the market for licit trade while seeking to disrupt counterfeit and substandard trade, and tax fraud.[1]

Strengthening policy co-ordination. Responsibility for addressing alcohol policy is typically shared by a number of ministries, all of whom should be involved in policymaking on licit and illicit trade. This would include, for example, customs, tax authorities, health and regulatory bodies, and authorities dealing with counterfeiting issues and other forms of illicit trade. These agencies must also be well-resourced for monitoring, intercepting, and deterring illicit activities throughout the entire supply chain. Areas for cross-agency co-ordination include: regulating and controlling the supply of raw materials, particularly ethanol; monitoring production sites, and requiring health and sanitary permits for manufacturers; strengthening national borders and law enforcement departments to identify and prevent illicit activity.

Engaging stakeholders. In-depth dialogue with private stakeholders must continue, as public-private partnerships are a promising tool for modern governance. Governments, civil society, communities, and businesses should work together to support a thriving, responsible, well-regulated business sector that supports sustainable growth, development, and a shared commitment to reduce the illicit alcohol trade.

Enhancing international co-operation. The WCO and law enforcement agencies already co-operate closely on illicit alcohol trade, and the OECD's Task Force on Illicit Trade plays an important role in bringing stakeholders together to discuss policy issues. Such co-operation needs to continue, and should include efforts to identify, discuss and promote "best practices".

Strengthening enforcement. Illicit players often continue to operate with relative impunity because of limited co-ordination and enforcement and penalties that are not significant enough to act as deterrents. Effective enforcement is needed to strengthen co-ordination among countries (to prevent counterfeiting or smuggling), among different national government agencies (to align fiscal, health and security priorities) and among different levels of government (federal, state, and municipal to ensure consistency and to mitigate potential corruption). Better tools and techniques for disrupting this trade need to be explored. Governments should also work on improving and digitalising customs mechanisms..

Awareness raising and consumer behaviour. Many consumers unknowingly buy illicit products, while others do so deliberately, for a variety of reasons. For those consumers who are deceived, public policies need to focus on raising awareness of the existence of illicit products and the associated harms. At the same time, consumers can be educated on how to distinguish licit products from illicit ones. Local knowledge and partnerships can be especially beneficial here.

Last, the analysis presented identifies several research areas that might merit further investigation. A more in-depth analysis of these topics could be beneficial for developing efficient enforcement and governance frameworks to counter the risks posed by illicit trade in alcohol:

- Enhancing information collection. There are numerous examples of the adverse effects that illicit alcohol has on public health, safety and on the environment. These examples, however, have limited scope. A more systematic and extensive approach for developing data in this area is therefore needed.

- Evidence on criminal dynamics. There are indications that networks that drive illicit alcohol trade are very dynamic. This is complicated by the COVID-19 pandemic, which has reinforced dynamism. Further investigation into how these dynamics evolve is needed, taking into account the interplay between corruption, enforcement gaps and illicit alcohol trade.

- Focus on best practices. There are a number of efforts employed by public and private stakeholders to counter illicit trade in alcohol. The issues for industry and policymakers to consider, presented above, give an indication of relevant policy areas. It could be useful to frame the existing best practices and examples of good governance.

Note

[1] See WHO (2019) "SAFER Technical Package," Availabe at: https://www.who.int/publications/i/item/the-safer-technical-package.

Annex A. IARD recommendations for addressing the challenges of unrecorded alcohol

1. The recommendations cover actions that governments, industry and the community can take (IARD, 2018).

Government

2. For illegal alcohol, including contraband, counterfeit items, products on which taxes have not been paid, and non-conforming alcohol, the association endorses: i) proportionate regulation of physical access and availability; ii) appropriate pricing policies that avoid extreme price differentials; iii) favourable fiscal incentives for production of affordable, safer alternatives; iv) monitoring and tracking of raw materials, notably denatured alcohol used in large-scale production; v) appropriate enforcement and controls in special trade or customs zones to prevent illegal activity; vi) aligning regulation across different sectors using denatured alcohol, medicinal potions and tinctures; vii) requirement for non-toxic denaturants or denaturants that change taste or colour with ethanol; viii) monetary incentive to return empties (preventing refills); and ix) improved collaboration between law enforcement and the justice system for effective prosecution and dismantling of organized trade in illegal alcohol.

3. For dealing with artisanal production issues, it is recommended that i) permits or registration be introduced where potential production volume is high (possibly with a tax exemption), ii) reuse of communal equipment be supported where home production is legal but unrecorded and iii) codes of practice be developed to establish standards for production and testing.

4. To discourage consumption of surrogate alcohol, i) limits could be established on the size of bottles to discourage the sale for purposes of consumption, ii) the packaging of surrogate alcohol should not lead to any confusion with alcohol, iii) sales of medical alcohol in pharmacies and other outlets could be limited and iii) use of ill-tasting denaturants in chemical solutions could be required.

Community

5. For the community, efforts concerning illegal alcohol should focus on improving education and social control around unrecorded alcohol: i) anonymous reporting of illegal production facilities and counterfeits in outlets should be encouraged; ii) public education and media campaigns focused on the nature of illegal activities should be pursued, iii) public education and media campaigns on the potential harms to health and potential poisoning from adulterated alcohol beverages should be developed, iv) awareness of the role that illicit activity plays in the market should be highlighted, and v) public education about new advances in labelling and packaging, to enable consumers to identify and avoid counterfeit alcohol should be supported.

6. For dealing with artisanal production issues, it is recommended that i) community education about safety and integrity standards and quality be endorsed, ii) cooperatives for production of village alcohol be supported, iii) competitions for (legal) home producers should be developed to

encourage quality standards and iv) community policing and enforcement of order around establishments should be pursued where these are unregulated and out of bounds for law enforcement.

7. For surrogate alcohol, i) community education about the dangers of consuming non-potable products should be advanced and ii) support should be given to indigent and marginalized social groups.

Industry

8. For industry, efforts in the area of illegal alcohol, this would include i) co-operation with law enforcement and customs, ii) intelligence sharing, iii) support for the development of standards in denaturation across different industries, iv) support for spot-checking and quality control of alcohol in serving establishments, v) development innovation in labelling and closures and "smart bottles", vi) support for original bottle collection by legal businesses and vii) technical innovation in authentication techniques.

9. For dealing with artisanal production issues, i) support for the testing of products and ii) education for home producers on safety and quality production techniques.

10. For surrogate alcohol, support for Legal purchase ages for sales of cough medicines and other alcohol-containing products, ii) ensuring that the packaging of surrogate alcohol does not lead to any confusion with alcohol, iii) monitoring of denatured alcohol along the value chain, and iii) support for use of non-toxic denaturants by chemical, pharmaceutical and cosmetics companies.